We Love to Craft
Christmas

Fun Stuff for Kids

17 Handmade Fabric & Paper Projects

Annabel Wrigley

FunStitch
S T U D I O
stitch your art out.

Text copyright © 2015 by Annabel Wrigley

Photography and artwork copyright © 2015 by C&T Publishing, Inc.

Publisher: Amy Marson

Creative Director: Gailen Runge

Art Director/Page Layout Artist:
Kristy Zacharias

Editor: Liz Aneloski

Technical Editors: Nan Powell and
Gailen Runge

Cover/Book Designer: April Mostek

Production Coordinator/Illustrator:
Jenny Davis

Production Editor: Katie Van Amburg

Photo Assistant: Mary Peyton Peppo

Style photography by Kristen Gardner
and instructional photography by
Diane Pedersen, unless otherwise noted

Published by FunStitch Studio, an imprint of C&T Publishing, Inc., P.O. Box 1456, Lafayette, CA 94549

Library of Congress Cataloging-in-Publication Data

Wrigley, Annabel, 1972-

We love to craft--Christmas : fun stuff for kids--17 handmade fabric & paper projects / Annabel Wrigley.

   pages cm

Audience: 8 to 14.

ISBN 978-1-61745-067-9 (soft cover)

1. Handicraft--Juvenile literature. 2. Christmas decorations--Juvenile literature. I. Title.

TT900.C4W755 2015

745.594'12--dc23

2014049833

Printed in China

10 9 8 7 6 5 4 3 2 1

DEDICATION

For Grescha

ACKNOWLEDGMENTS

It's crazy to think that I'm here again, with my fourth book in four years. It has been an absolute joy to create these books for all my young crafty friends all over the world.

I was so excited to get the opportunity to work on a Christmas book that would include some fun crafts as well as sewing projects.

To Roxane Cerda: Thank you so much for coming to me with this idea. I knew instantly that it would be a project that I would love working on, and it truly has been so fun!

To Liz Aneloski: You have such a calming influence over me when I am feeling a wee bit frazzled. You are such a wonderful editor! Thank you.

To everyone at C&T Publishing: I feel like you are all my "other family," and I am so proud to be a part of this amazing imprint!

To National Nonwovens (woolfelt.com) and Copenhagen Print factory (copenhagenprintfactory.com): A huge thank-you for the great products.

To Kate Mckean: Knowing that I have someone to help me, support me, and go to bat for me has gotten me to where I am today. Thank you. You are the best!

To Darren, Ollie, and Ruby, my amazing family: I could never have done this again without you. Darren, you have become a pretty stellar cook. … I may just need to do another book so I have an excuse to let you cook for me more often!

Gosh, where would I be without all my lovely students?! I want to thank you all for all the enthusiasm and inspiration you give me on a daily basis. I am so lucky to be able to do this job and work with all of you amazing kids. #bestjobever

CONTENTS

PROJECTS

A NOTE FROM COURTNEY CERRUTI

Placing ornaments on the tree felt special—magical, even.

Every year at Christmastime, my brother and I reached into the box of carefully wrapped ornaments, delicately plucking one from its honeycomb housing as we decorated the tree. With the fire blazing and Frank Sinatra on the stereo, my parents told stories about certain ornaments as they recalled previous Christmases, sharing memories foreign to us. Ornaments that my brother and I made when we were young children evoked snippets of stories about us in preschool or kindergarten and Christmas mornings we couldn't remember. As we added tiny gold-winged angels, glittered fruits, and small animals to the tree, the fire burned, the box became empty, and eventually the four of us were left standing in the glow of the adorned and sparkling tree.

For me, decorating the Christmas tree was the one part of the season that was calm and where we came together as a family. Exchanging presents was a whirl of tattered paper and excited shouts as we tore open gifts and cast others aside. But placing ornaments on the tree felt special—magical, even.

As an adult, I still decorate the tree with my parents when I'm home for Christmas. The salt-dough boy, painted in watercolor and glazed with glue, reminds me of my piano lessons and a teacher who made crafts with us and gave us prizes when we learned new songs. I think of the 30-plus Christmases I've shared with my family. These handmade artifacts that decorate our tree every year tell the story of my family and our holiday traditions.

Annabel's book, *We Love to Craft— Christmas*, embodies the spirit of the season, evoking the same feeling I get every Christmas when my mom dusts off the giant box of ornaments and we stand, ready and waiting, to decorate this year's tree.

Her beautifully curated projects are heirloom pieces that can be created by children and enjoyed by all. Her approach to the creative process empowers girls to make design choices while strengthening their skills in achievable projects they can be proud of.

—Courtney Cerruti

CHRISTMAS LOVE

Christmas has always been my favorite time of the year—I'm not sure if it's all about being with family, or maybe it's just my love of tradition, but I'm a total sucker for all things festive.

I have lived in Virginia for about 12 years and have grown to love my white Christmases, but nothing beats a stifling hot Christmas with plum pudding and some serious beach time in my native Australia.

We never really decorated much at Christmas. It was hard to get a fresh tree, but my mother always decorated the loveliest fake tree. I always looked forward to pulling out the bits and bobs from the cupboard—from tiny Santas to sparkling reindeer. There is really something about Christmas decorating that makes everyone feel happy and excited!

I was excited to have the opportunity to work on a book all about Christmas, just for you. I hope you find something just perfect to craft and sew this holiday season.

Maybe you could start your own Christmas tradition.

You don't need to limit these projects to the holidays either! Change the fabrics and make things for all year-round!

HOW TO USE THIS BOOK

Every project in this book should be easy enough for you to complete; however, some are more challenging than others. We don't want it to be too easy, right? *That would be boring!*

You will notice that each project has a little symbol beside it. These symbols have different meanings. Here is what they mean.

NO SEW

This means that this project is purely a craft project with no sewing required!

EASY PEASY

These are great projects to start with if you have not had a lot of experience with the sewing machine, if you are new to the world of crafting and sewing, or if you want a quicker project.

A TEENY BIT MORE CHALLENGING

These are great projects for those of you with a little more confidence. You will be sewing a lot more with the machine, so it's important to be able to sew in a straight line.

TAKE YOUR TIME AND ASK FOR HELP

These projects are the most challenging, but they're certainly not so difficult that you can't get them done! All you need is some patience and perseverance. These projects are for girls who have some experience with a sewing machine and want to try something that's a little more challenging. Remember: it's totally fine to ask an adult for help if you need it.

Tips for Successful Sewing and Crafting

Like most things, when it comes to sewing and crafting, it's better to take your time before you embark on a new project. Jumping in without proper preparation can sometimes lead to frustration and a tangled knotty mess!

Keep Your Cool

In all my books I talk about the importance of staying cool, calm, and collected. Sewing and crafting should be fun and relaxing, but sometimes you may feel pressure to finish a project in record time or before anyone else. Remember: you're more likely to make mistakes if you speed. You don't want to spend all your time pulling out wonky stitches. Take your time to make your project look as good as possible. If you are working with a friend, sew at your own speed.

There is nothing more beautiful than the pride you will feel after you finish a project of your own.

tip Practice makes perfect! Take some time to practice on some of the easier projects; that will help give you confidence to tackle some of the harder projects.

Practice Makes Confidence

When any new students come to my studio, I always make them start sewing with the same exercise. It may seem boring, but it's the best way to get a feel for your sewing machine and to learn about speed control.

Embrace Your Creativity

This book gives you the opportunity to express yourself through your fabric and color choices. Don't think for a second that you have to stick to reds and greens and holiday colors! Feel free to substitute any colors or patterns you love. It is your project and it is up to you to decide how the finished product will look.

Here is my favorite practice exercise.

1.

2.

3.

Draw some lines on a solid-colored piece of fabric. I use FriXion erasable markers because the lines can be removed by ironing with a warm iron.

Thread your sewing machine with bright-colored thread that you can easily see on the piece of fabric.

Start at the top of the line and sew all the way to the bottom of the line, making sure to stay on the line as best you can. Work hard to maintain an even foot pressure; it's easy to get overconfident and sew too fast! When you sew fast, it's hard to stay on the line.

4. & 5.

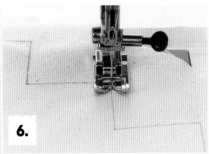

6.

Keep sewing lines until you feel confident in your straight sewing. When you have finished the lines, turn over the fabric and line up the edge of the presser foot with a stitch line.

Sew down each line, making sure to keep the edge of the presser foot running along the stitch line. All the sewing projects in this book use a ⅜″ seam allowance, and with many machines, this is the width of the presser foot.

If you feel that straight sewing is getting really easy, try drawing some wavy and jagged lines. These are a lot harder to sew on, but they are great practice for turning corners and sewing slowly. Take your time and try not to get frustrated, and you'll be amazed at what you can do.

WHAT WILL I NEED?

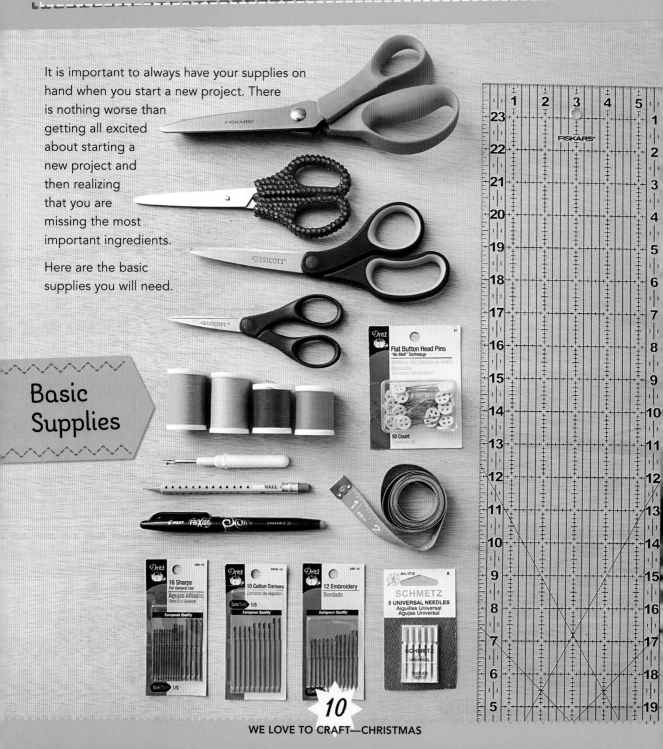

It is important to always have your supplies on hand when you start a new project. There is nothing worse than getting all excited about starting a new project and then realizing that you are missing the most important ingredients.

Here are the basic supplies you will need.

Basic Supplies

WE LOVE TO CRAFT—CHRISTMAS

Sewing Machine

Many of the projects in this book will require you to use a sewing machine. A relative or friend may have one, or you may have one. Do you feel comfortable sewing on the sewing machine by yourself? If you are not quite sure, take the time to find the manual that came with your sewing machine. It's okay if you can't find it; you should be able to download one for your particular sewing machine from the Internet. You can also take a look on YouTube. There are so many wonderful things you can find online!

Sewing Machine Needles

You can't sew on your sewing machine without having a sharp sewing machine needle!

I know it can sometimes be confusing trying to figure out which needle to choose for your sewing machine. I recommend that you use only universal needles. The little packet will say "universal needles" on the front, and you'll need to use only a size 12 or 14 for the fabrics that we will be sewing.

Pins

Pins are very important for you to have on hand at all times. They are so important to hold your work together for sewing. At the moment I am really loving flat plastic flower-head or button-top pins. I love the longer length; it is perfect for all my sewing projects.

Hand-Sewing Needles

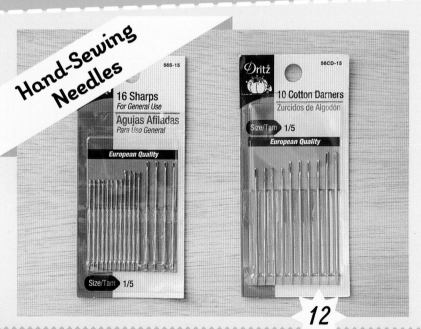

There are a couple of projects in this book that will require you to do some hand sewing. It's always important to have a few hand-sewing needles available in different sizes.

Embroidery Needles

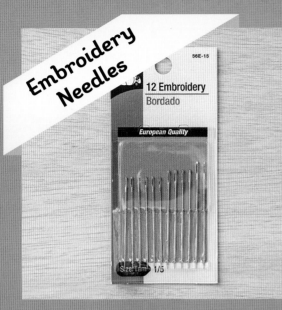

Embroidery needles are wonderful because they are a little longer and have a larger eye, so they are great to use with embroidery floss or perle cotton.

Ruler

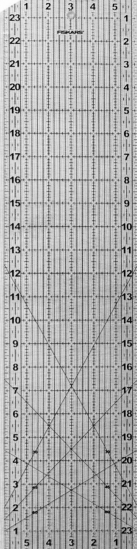

Rulers come in all shapes and sizes and are essential to create those super-straight lines for cutting. I always have a clear 6½″ × 24″ acrylic quilter's ruler on hand. It is great for measuring and for cutting fabric strips.

Tape Measure

Trying to measure a curve with a straight ruler can give you a headache! Always have a tape measure handy to measure those awkwardly shaped or super-long things!

Scissors

There is nothing worse than trying to cut fabric with a dull pair of scissors. Make sure you have a good pair of scissors for cutting fabric, another pair for cutting paper, and a small pair for detailed cutting. Pinking shears come in handy to finish raw edges.

I usually mark my scissors with a piece of twine or tape so I remember to use my fabric scissors only for cutting fabric.

Seam Ripper

We all make mistakes, right? This nifty little tool is wonderful for pulling out those wonky stitches. Think of it as a wonky stitch eraser. Simply slide the sharp end under the wonky stitch in question, and the little curved blade will snip the stitch without snipping the fabric as well.

Erasable Pen

I always have to have a couple of erasable pens on hand when I am working on a project. Sometimes being able to draw a stitch line or a few notes on my fabric can make all the difference. I love the Pilot FriXion pens. All you have to do to remove the ink is apply the heat of a hot iron. It really is like magic!

SEWING MACHINE

Don't be scared off by all the knobs and buttons on your sewing machine. It may be a piece of machinery, but it is certainly nothing to be afraid of. I have seen some sewing students come to class totally afraid of the sewing machine and then leave sewing like a pro.

Always make sure you are fully prepared before you sit down at your sewing machine. Make sure you've had a good look through the sewing machine manual and that you've done a little bit of sewing practice on a plain piece of fabric. It's always good to do a little practice and try out all the dials and buttons before you start working on your special fabric.

Threading the Sewing Machine

I have worked with a lot of different sewing machines, and there is one thing they all have in common: they all need to be threaded correctly in order to work. Sounds easy, right? Well, it usually is, but sometimes we need a bit of practice to get the machine threaded perfectly.

Most modern machines are threaded in a similar way, but some of those adorable old machines are super complicated and will need a little more

practice. This is the time to pull out the manual and ask for help if you need it.

I've had many occasions when a student has been sewing and we heard a loud clunk. It's amazing the terrible noise a sewing machine can make if it is threaded incorrectly. Always make sure it is threaded correctly the first time; you'll be glad you did!

The Importance of Sewing Machine Needles

Always make sure you have a full pack of sewing needles on hand when you start a new project. It's frustrating not to have a replacement if you break a needle midway through a project and have to go to the store for a packet. You may live far away from a sewing store, and this can be a real headache. Even when you are sewing as carefully as you can, needles can break if you accidentally hit a pin or try sewing through a particularly thick piece of fabric.

To change the needle, follow these steps:

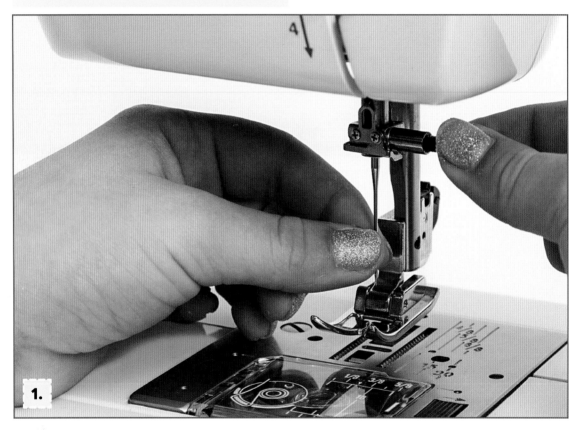

1.

Loosen the little screw right beside the needle. Most machines will have a little screwdriver in the toolbox, or you sometimes may be able to unscrew the screw with your fingers.

2.

tip Always make sure to dispose of your used and broken sewing needles safely. Those little sharp ends of the broken needle are super hard to see and very painful to step on! So make sure that you put the needle in the garbage can right away.

Remove the old needle and replace it with a new one.

3.

Tighten the screw as tightly as you can.

The Parts of Your Sewing Machine

I think it's important that you have a good understanding of all the different parts of your sewing machine before you start a project. There are no doubt some buttons on your sewing machine you're not 100% sure about. I thought it might help if I showed each one to you.

Tension control

This is really important. This dial controls the tension or tightness of the top thread. Usually if your stitching looks a little strange, it is because of the tension. Look at your manual or ask an adult for help if you are confused.

Thread take-up lever

This part of the machine helps you keep the correct thread tension as you sew. If your machine is not sewing properly or makes a loud thumping sound, it may be because the thread has become unthreaded from the take-up lever.

Stitch length selector

This is the dial you turn to choose how long your stitch length will be. A stitch length of 2.5 is a good standard setting for your machine. Your machine may have a different number or dial; play around with it to find a good even-sized stitch, not too big and not too small. Sometimes there is just a dial with different stitch lengths to choose from. You should turn it to a medium-sized stitch.

Handwheel

This round wheel at the end of the machine is the way to manually lift the needle up and down.

Presser foot lifter

This lever on your machine is in control of lifting and lowering the presser foot. Make sure to always have the presser foot down for sewing.

Feed dogs

These are like little hands that push the fabric under the presser foot. They keep the fabric moving without you having to push or pull it.

Presser feet

Most sewing machines come with a selection of presser feet to be used for all different sewing projects. In this book we will be using a regular sewing foot. We sometimes call the presser foot a chicken foot. It kind of looks like one, don't you think?

Reverse button

This is the little button you will need to press or push down to make the machine sew backward. Remember that whenever you start sewing, you should backstitch at the beginning and end.

LET'S CHOOSE FABRICS

There are so many fun holiday fabrics to choose from.

Check your local thrift shop for fun old holiday linens and clothes that you can cut up and reuse in your holiday projects. These are the main fabrics I use for my projects.

Choosing fabrics certainly is the most fun part of embarking on a new project—you can really inject your personality into your choice of fabrics and colors and patterns. Most fabric stores sell a great variety of holiday prints! Remember that you don't always have to get a holiday-themed fabric to make your projects look holiday-esque. There are lots of great polka dots and stripes that can help complement your Christmas projects.

Cotton Fabric

Cotton fabric comes in many fun colors and designs for the holidays. It's a great weight, it's easily washable, and it's super easy to work with. Some of the projects work better with a heavier cotton fabric. This is the time to go to the decorator section of your fabric store and look for some slightly heavier fabrics. I particularly like these heavier fabrics for pillow projects.

Felt

Wool felt is my all-time favorite—it comes in a zillion different colors, it feels beautiful, it's easy to work with, and best of all it doesn't fray. All these reasons make it perfect for many of the projects in this book. There are some great synthetic felt choices out there too, but just be aware that you will always have to use a pressing cloth when you're ironing synthetic felt, because it can easily burn and melt with the heat of an iron.

I love felt! I will admit it: I think I may be a felt-aholic!

WHAT SPECIAL SKILLS DO I NEED?

Near the beginning of most of the projects, you will see a section called Special Skills. Some of the things listed may be skills you already have, and some may be new skills that you need to master before you start the project. Remember that you can always come back to this section if you need to brush up on your special skills.

Using Pins

Sewing a new project can be made so much easier if you know how to use pins correctly. Pins are important to keep two or more pieces of fabric together, so they don't move when you sew. Sometimes pinning may seem like it takes a lot of time when all you want to do is just start a project, but I promise it will be worth your while when you see how great and neat your work will look after it's been pinned correctly.

My favorite way to pin is with the pins perpendicular to the edge of the fabric. I prefer it this way because the pins are easier to remove as I sew along. I always like to keep a little pincushion beside me when I'm working, so I can keep the pins out of the way after I remove them.

Sewing Around a Corner

There are a couple of projects in this book that will require you to sew around a corner. This is an important skill to learn so your corners look neat as a pin.

Here Is How to Do It

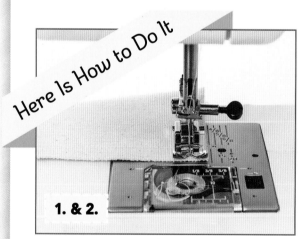

1. & 2.

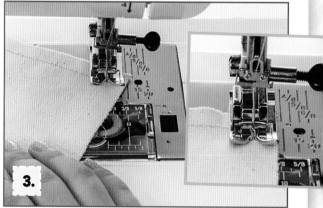

3.

Sew down the edge of your work and stop about a presser-foot width from the corner.

Turn the handwheel so the needle is in the fabric.

While the needle is still in the fabric, lift the presser foot and turn the fabric in the direction you need to go to sew the next edge.

Easy, right?

Using a Hot Glue Gun

Hot glue guns are the greatest invention! There is only one bad thing about them: **they are very hot!**

Make sure you use only a low-temperature hot glue gun; you will really save yourself a lot of nasty burns on your fingers.

Always make sure that you have a non-meltable surface to position your glue gun on! In other words, not on your family's best dining table!

Using an Iron

Ironing can make the difference between your project looking kind of good and looking amazingly awesome. It really is the perfect way to make your project look polished and finished.

Make sure to ask an adult for some help when you are ironing for the first time. I'm sure you're a little impatient to get started, but taking the time to ask for help will really help you have a successful ironing experience. Be sure to keep your body and your fingers out of the way when you are ironing.

Always check the fabric you are using; some fabrics are made of synthetic fibers and can melt if you use an iron that is too hot. This is a good time to ask for help if you're not sure.

I know it can be fun to press that steam button, but you can get a nasty burn if your hands get in the way of the steam. Ask for help if you are not sure where the steam button is located on your iron.

I personally like to turn off the steam and use a water spray bottle on the fabric before I iron. It helps my fabric stay super smooth.

23

Using Parchment Paper to Make Templates

Most of the projects in this book have patterns that you will need to trace to make template pieces. A template is essentially a pattern piece. The instructions for each project will tell you which page the pattern pieces can be found on.

All the pattern pieces are the right size for you to trace and use. You won't need to go to a copier and enlarge or reduce any of the patterns—that is, unless you decide you want to make some of the projects bigger or smaller!

My favorite type of tracing paper is the parchment paper that you find in the baking aisle of the supermarket. It's super inexpensive, and you probably even have a roll at home.

Here Is How to Do It

1.

Lay parchment or tracing paper over the pattern and trace the shape with a sharp pencil. Be sure to add all the markings. It will usually say on the pattern piece how many pieces you should be cutting and which fabric they should be cut from. Be sure to add all these markings to your template; it will make things a lot easier later on.

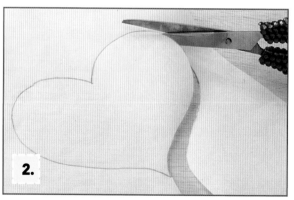

2.

Cut out the template. Be sure to cut carefully!

Using Paper-Backed Fusible Web

I always have a large roll of fusible web on hand for all the projects we make in the studio. It's a wonderful product to use when you need to attach one fabric to another without having to pin, like in our Sweet Deer Pillow project (page 32).

My favorite type of fusible web is HeatnBond Lite.

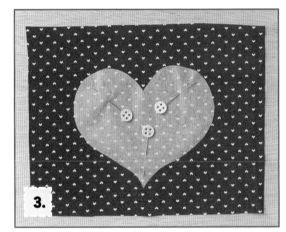

3.

Pin the template to the piece of fabric that you are cutting.

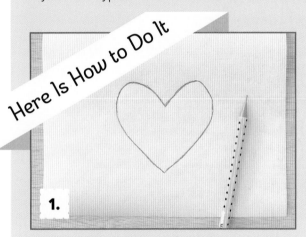

Here Is How to Do It

1.

Trace or draw the shape that you need on the paper side of a piece of fusible web. A pencil is best for this, as erasable marker will come off when you iron the web to the fabric.

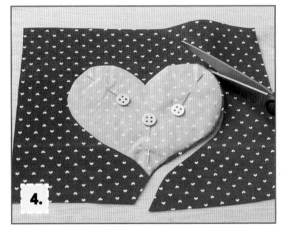

4.

Carefully cut around the fabric.

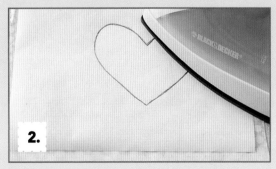

2.

Turn off the steam on the iron and iron the fusible web to the wrong side of the fabric.

3.

4.

When the fabric has cooled down, cut out the shape.

Peel off the backing paper.

Using Fusible Interfacing

Some of the projects in this book require fusible interfacing to make the fabrics feel a little bit stiffer. I like to use featherweight fusible interfacing, which is easily found in your local craft store.

Fusible interfacing has two sides. One is a little bumpy and one is smooth. The bumpy side is the side with the glue attached.

5.

Position the shape on your fabric and iron it in place. If you are using synthetic felt or fabric, always lay a piece of scrap fabric over the shape before you iron to prevent the fabric from melting.

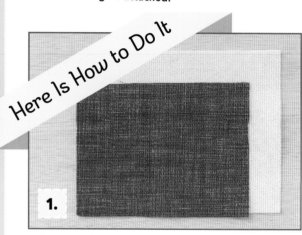

Here Is How to Do It

1.

When you have cut the pattern piece from the fabric, lay it on top of the fusible interfacing, with the glue side facing up.

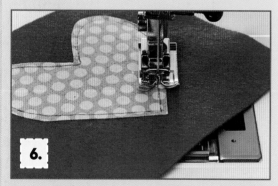

6.

Sew nice and close to the edge around the shape. You can use an erasable pen to draw a stitch line if you need help making your stitches nice and even.

2.

Cut around the interfacing.

3.

Use a hot iron over the fabric until the interfacing is well fused to the fabric.

Making a Pom-Pom

I think this super-special skill is one of the most important skills to know—I mean, who doesn't love a pom-pom?

Here Is How to Do It

1.

Wrap the yarn around the widest part of your hand about 75 to 100 times. If you're using thick yarn you can probably use half that amount. Be sure not to wrap it too tightly; you don't want to cut off the circulation in your fingers.

2. & 3.

Carefully slide the yarn bundle off your hand, making sure to keep it all together.

Cut an extra piece of yarn and wrap it around the middle of the yarn bundle.

4.

Tie a knot as tightly as you can.

5.

Use a sharp pair of scissors to cut all the loops.

6.

Trim the entire pom-pom into a round shape. The more you trim it the thicker it will look.

What Special Skills Do I Need?

Here Is How to Make a
MULTICOLORED POM-POM

1 Wrap yarn around your hand about 20 times.

2 Add a second color by wrapping another 20 times with a different color of yarn.

3 Continue this way with as many colors as you like.

4 Tie and trim the pom-pom just as before. Look how amazing it looks!

SEWING TERMS

There may be words in this book that you've never heard before. They're all pretty simple, though, and I'm here to explain them all to you.

Backstitch

It is a really good habit to backstitch at the beginning and end of every stitch line. This creates a strong beginning and ending that prevents the stitches from coming undone. Most sewing machines have a backward or back-stitch button. Some are buttons you press and some are levers you hold down.

Having trouble finding it? Pull out your sewing machine manual and take a look; it will tell you where everything is.

When you start sewing a seam, sew a few stitches forward and then press or hold down the backstitch button for a couple of stitches. Let go of the button and continue forward until you get to the end of the stitch line. When you reach the end, hold or press down the backstitch button and go backward again to secure the stitches.

Sew with the Presser Foot on the Edge of the Fabric

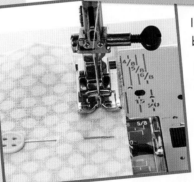

I say this a lot in all the projects, but it's really, really important!

Most sewing machines come with a regular presser foot that is ⅜″ wide. This means it's ⅜″ from the center of the foot to the edge. That is why the projects in this book use a ⅜″ seam allowance. In other words, most of the projects can simply be sewn with the edge of the presser foot on the edge of the fabric. Make sure that the very edge of the presser foot is perfectly lined up with the raw edge of the fabric.

seam note

The seam allowance for most projects in this book is ⅜″. If your presser foot only measures ¼″, use a piece of washi or masking tape as a guide to help line everything up. Sew with the edge of the fabric on the edge of the tape. Place the inner edge of the tape ⅜″ out from the machine's needle.

Seam

The seam is the stitching line that you have just sewn to join one piece of fabric to another piece of fabric.

Seam Allowance

This is the measurement from the stitch line to the edge of the fabric. It is super important to always follow the correct seam allowance for your projects. This will make all the project pieces fit together perfectly. The seam allowance for most of the projects in this book is ⅜″. See Seam Note (page 29).

Clipping the Curves

Sometimes when you sew a project that has lots of curves (like the Stitchy Striped Christmas Stocking, page 86) and needs to be turned right side out, you will need to clip the curves to make the project super flat and neat and to keep the curves extra curvy.

Right before you turn the project right side out, take a sharp pair of scissors and carefully snip a little slit in the fabric about every ½″. Be sure not to clip the stitching.

30

Right Side of the Fabric

You will probably read about placing fabric with right sides together. This simply means placing the fabric with the right sides facing each other … or as I often say to my students, "with the pretty sides kissing"!

Fat Quarter

A fat quarter is a piece of fabric that measures around 18″ × 20″. Most fabric and quilt shops sell fat quarters. They are the perfect size for small projects and are super affordable.

Selvage

The selvage is the finished (nonfraying) edge down the side of the fabric, where there are usually details of the fabric designer. It is often white but can also be other colors.

C 6175 Mini Dots

Sweet Deer Pillow

If you are using a ¼″ presser foot, don't forget to use washi tape as a guide to make the correct seam allowance width for this project (see Seam Note, page 29).

what do i need?

* ¾ yard of 54″-wide decorator-weight fabric in fun holiday print OR 1¼ yards of 40″-wide quilting cotton

* 8″ × 10″ piece of fusible web

* 8″ × 10″ piece of wool felt (Synthetic felt is another option.)

* 20″ × 20″ pillow form

* Erasable pen (I use FriXion erasable markers because they erase with the heat of an iron.)

* Basic sewing supplies

note

If you are using synthetic felt, be sure to use a pressing cloth when you iron, so you do not melt the felt.

special skills

* Using pins (page 22)

* Sewing around a corner (page 22)

* Using an iron (page 23)

* Using templates (page 24)

* Using fusible web (page 25)

* PREPARE the Pieces

* Using the Sweet Deer Pillow pattern (on pattern pullout page P2), trace the deer design to the paper side of the fusible web.

* Cut 1 piece of fabric to measure 20″ × 20″ for the pillow front.

* Cut 2 pieces of fabric to measure 15″ × 20″ for the pillow back.

I love to decorate my space with fun and pretty pillows. With this easy sewing project, you can make a whole stack (or herd) of sweet deer holiday pillows, *just perfect for your festive space.*

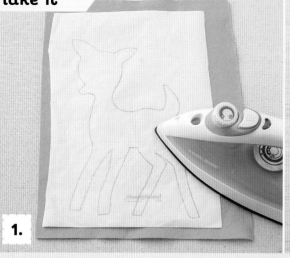

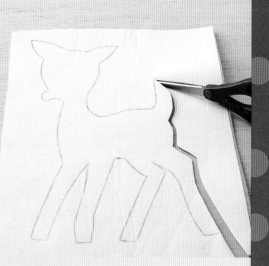

1.

Iron the traced fusible web to a piece of wool felt and then cut out the deer.

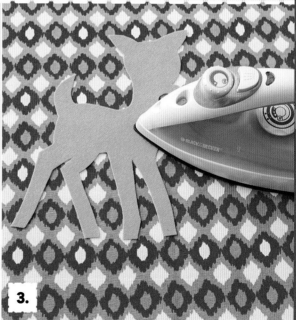

2.

Peel the backing fabric from the deer shape and place the deer on the right side of the pillow front, with the fusible side facing down.

3.

Carefully iron the deer in place. Take your time with this.

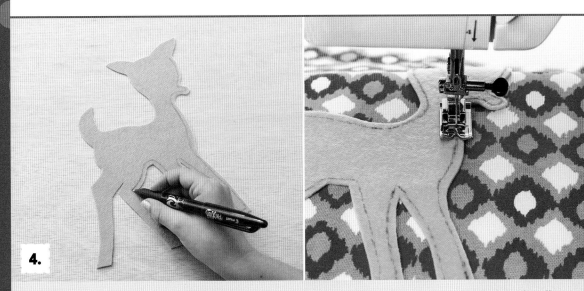

4.

Draw a line with an erasable pen about ⅛″ from the edge of the felt. Don't worry! The ink will come off with the iron. Sew around the deer, making sure to sew nice and close to the edge.

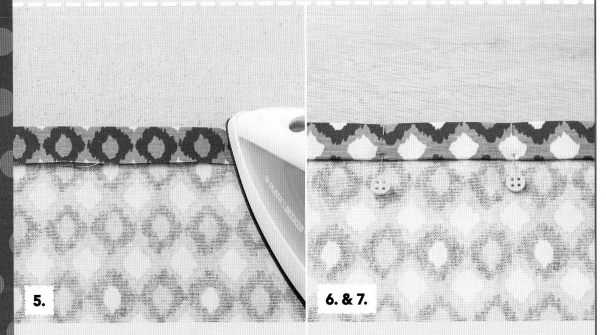

5.

Fold over a long edge of a pillow back piece ½″. Iron along this fold.

6. & 7.

Fold it over again, iron the fold, and pin it in place.

Repeat Steps 5 and 6 with the second back piece.

Sew down the fold on both pieces. Try to sew close to the edge of the first fold.

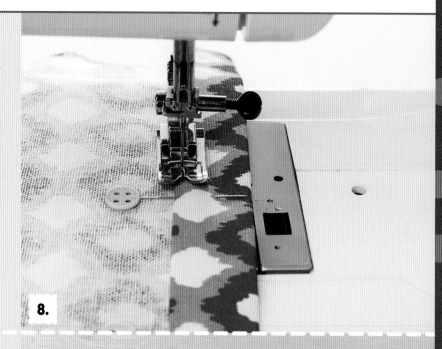

8.

Place the pillow front faceup on the table and lay a back piece facedown on top of the front piece. Be sure to line up the raw edges along the top, bottom, and 1 side.

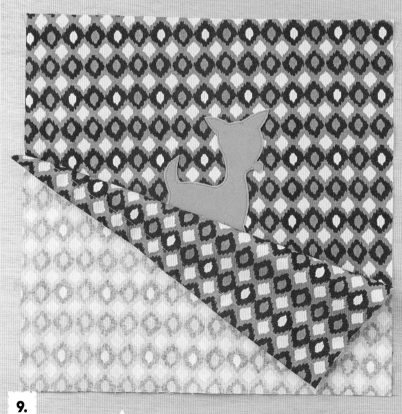

9.

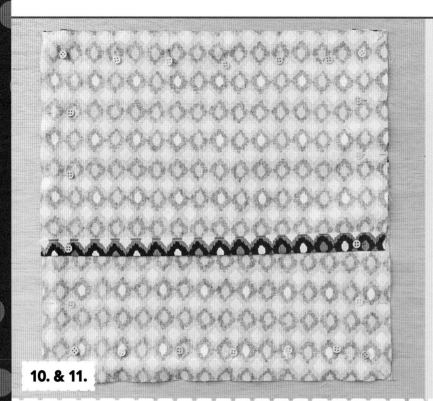

Now, lay the second back piece facedown on the stack. This time, make sure that the piece is lined up with the other side of the pillow front. The 2 back pieces will overlap, with the hemmed edges toward the center.

Pin everything in place.

10. & 11.

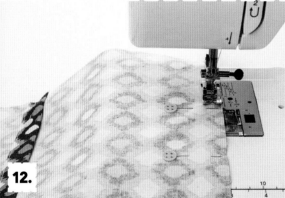

12.

Sew around all 4 sides, with the edge of the presser foot on the edge of the fabric. Take care sewing around those corners!

13. – 15.

Trim all the corners and trim around the edges with pinking shears to prevent fraying (be careful not to cut the stitching!). Turn the pillow right side out.

Iron the pillow cover.

Insert the pillow form and admire the result of all your hard work!

Fabric-Wrapped Gift

what do i need?

* Gift to wrap

* Piece of fabric
  (The size will depend on the size of your gift.)

* Tape measure

* Scissors

note

Make sure your fabric piece is wide enough to fold up both sides of the gift and that it measures around 5 times the length of the gift.

LET'S Wrap It

1. Fold both of the long edges so that they overlap on top of the gift.

2. Fold in the long end on each side to make the ends a little easier to tie.

3. & 4.

Pull the ties up and tie in a knot on top of the gift. Carefully fold in any loose fabric bits.

Add a fun homemade gift tag and ribbon and give this sweet gift—no tape needed!

We always think of paper when it comes time to wrap a special gift. *Have you ever thought of using fabric?* You may have a fabric print you just know your friend will love to bits. The best part is that the wrapping can be made into a super-sweet sewing project afterward.

Take your time
and ask for
help

Felt Forest Tree Skirt

what do i need?

* At least 45˝ × 45˝ piece of canvas drop cloth or cotton print fabric

* At least 45˝ × 45˝ piece of cotton quilt batting

* At least 45˝ × 45˝ piece of fun cotton fabric (Decorator-weight fabric is usually around 54˝ wide, or sew 2 pieces of regular cotton fabric together.)

* Several sheets of felt in 3 different greens

* 1 sheet of red felt

* Erasable pen (I use FriXion erasable markers because they erase with the heat of an iron.)

* Liquid Stitch fabric glue

* Basic sewing supplies

special skills

* Using pins (page 22)

* Sewing around a corner (page 22)

* Using an iron (page 23)

* Using templates (page 24)

PREPARE the Pieces

* Cut a piece of drop cloth or print fabric, a piece of batting, and a piece of cotton fabric to all measure 45˝ × 45˝.

* Cut a variety of trees and houses from green and red felt (see patterns, page 47).

If you are using a ¼˝ presser foot, don't forget to use washi tape as a guide to make the correct seam allowance width for this project (see Seam Note, page 29).

Give your Christmas tree the skirt it deserves with this super-cute tree skirt made from a paint drop cloth from the hardware store. Make it reversible so you can change it out year after year.

LET'S Make It

1.

Lay the drop cloth or fabric out on a large flat surface.

2.

Fold the square in half diagonally from corner to corner.

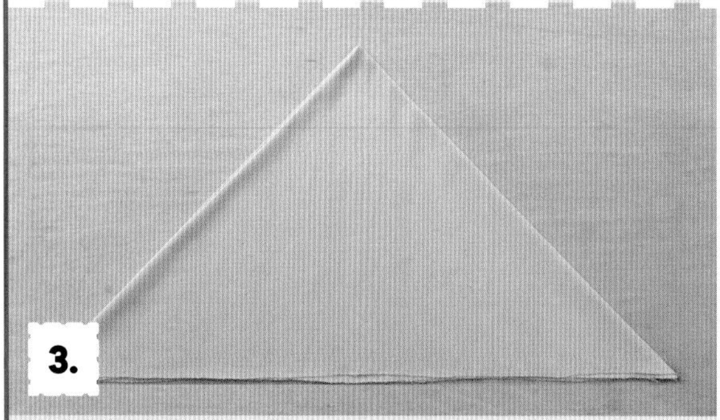

3.

Fold it in half again to make a large triangle.

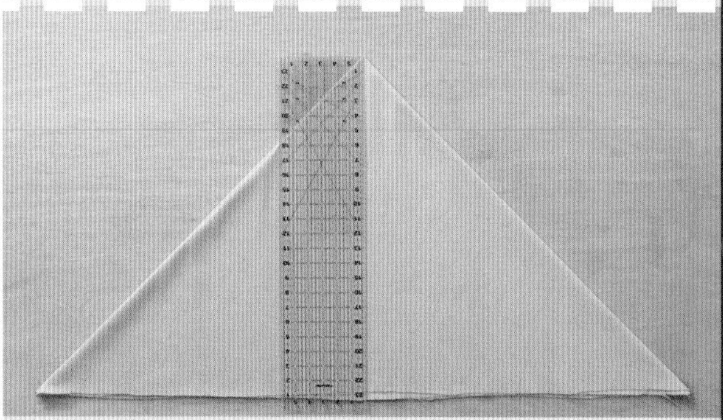

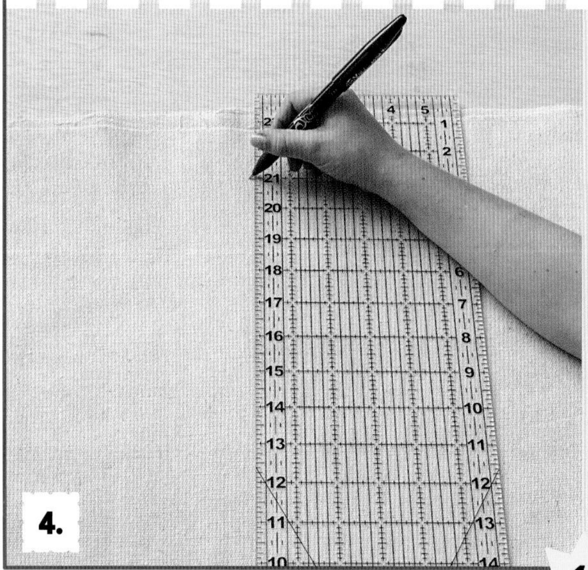

4.

Measure 21″ from the middle point of the triangle and mark with an erasable pen. Keeping the bottom of the ruler in place on the point, gently slide the ruler over and mark the 21″ spot with an erasable pen.

5.

Continue doing this all along to create an arc. Make sure to keep the bottom edge of the ruler in position the entire time. Carefully join the dots with an erasable pen.

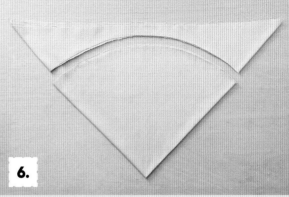

6.

Cut along the marked curve.

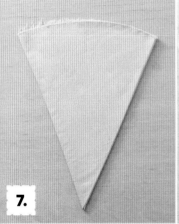

7.

Fold the triangle in half again.

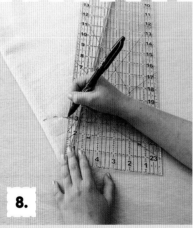

8.

Use the ruler to measure up 3″ from the triangle point. Mark the curve using the ruler in the same way that you did for the large circle.

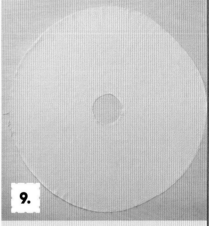

9.

Cut off the point along the drawn curve. Open out the circle; it will look like a giant doughnut!

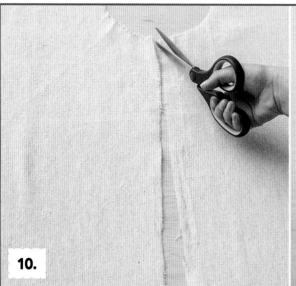

10.

Use a ruler to draw a straight line from the edge of the circle to the center. Cut along that line.

11.

Lay the batting on a flat surface.

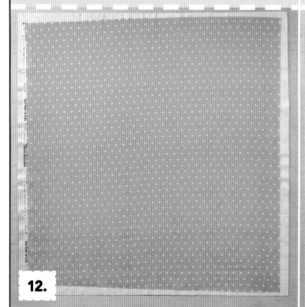

12.

Lay the backing fabric faceup on top of the batting.

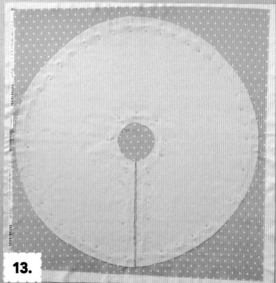

13.

Finally, lay the main skirt piece on top. A drop cloth doesn't have a right or wrong side, but if you are using a print you should place the print side facing down. Pin the pieces together.

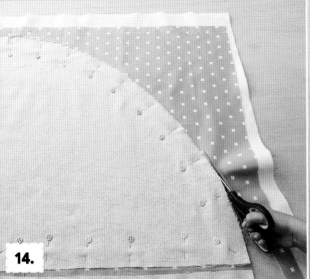

14.

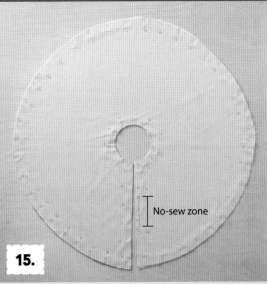

No-sew zone

15.

Cut around the skirt shape with a sharp pair of scissors.

Pin all the way around the skirt, including the inside circle. Mark a 5″ no-sew zone. This will be the area that we do not sew. We want to be able to turn the skirt right side out, right?

16.

17.

18.

Sew around the skirt with the edge of the presser foot on the edge of the fabric.

Trim the points off the corners (be careful not to cut the stitching!).

Clip the curves on the skirt (see Clipping the Curves, page 30) every inch or so in the seam allowance. This will help the curves stay nice and flat when you turn the piece right side out.

19.

Turn the skirt right side out. Be sure to pull it out from between the 2 fabric pieces rather than the batting and backing.

20.

Press the entire skirt well. Fold in the raw edges of the hole and pin the hole closed.

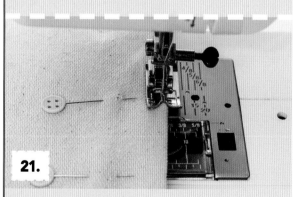

21.

Sew nice and close to the edge to close the hole.

FINISH
Up

1.

Lay out the tree design in a way that you love.

2.

Apply a line of fabric glue along the edge of a tree and glue it in place.

3. & 4.

Continue gluing on trees and houses until the tree skirt looks just the way you like it.

Give it a day to dry and set; then put it under the tree. It will be so pretty that you will hate to put gifts on top of it!

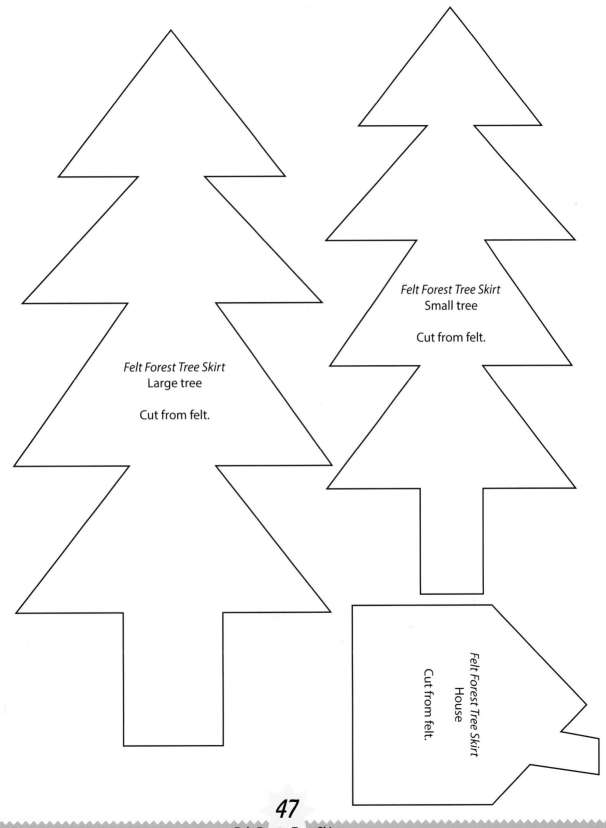

Felt Forest Tree Skirt
Large tree

Cut from felt.

Felt Forest Tree Skirt
Small tree

Cut from felt.

Felt Forest Tree Skirt
House
Cut from felt.

Easy peasy

Festive Holiday Crown

> If you are using a ¼″ presser foot, don't forget to use washi tape as a guide to make the correct seam allowance width for this project (see Seam Note, page 29).

what do i need?

* ¼ yard of quilting fabric for outside of crown

* ¼ yard of quilting fabric for inside of crown

* 24″ of fun ribbon, ½″–1″ wide

* ½ yard of featherweight fusible interfacing

* Erasable pen (I use FriXion erasable markers because they erase with the heat of an iron.)

* Basic sewing supplies

special skills

* Using pins (page 22)

* Sewing around a corner (page 22)

* Using an iron (page 23)

* Using templates (page 24)

* Using fusible interfacing (page 26)

PREPARE the Pieces

* Iron a piece of fusible interfacing to the wrong side of the outside crown fabric piece; then add a second layer of fusible interfacing on top of that. Do the same thing on the inside crown fabric.

* Use the crown pattern (on pattern pullout page P2) to trace and cut out 1 crown from each of the interfaced fabrics.

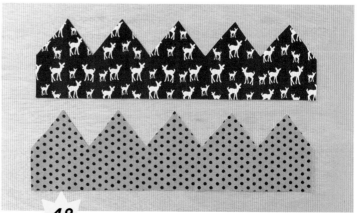

48

When I was growing up we would always sit around the table at Christmas proudly wearing the paper crowns that came in our crackers. The only problem was that after a few hours our paper hats would be in tatters. *Here is a fun crown that you can use year after year.*

1. & 2.

Measure 1″ from the bottom of the crown on each side of the front crown fabric piece and mark within an erasable pen.

Cut the piece of ribbon in half and pin a piece facing inward at the marked point on each side of the crown fabric front. The ribbons need to be pinned on the right side of the fabric.

3.

4.

Lay the crown fabric pieces right sides together and pin along the bottom straight edge of the crown and the straight lower sides. The ribbon will be encased inside.

Sew the straight lower sides and the bottom straight edge with the edge of the presser foot on the edge of the fabric (see Seam Note, page 29).

5.

6.

Trim the corners (be careful not to cut the stitches).

Turn the crown right side out and carefully press all the edges with the iron.

50

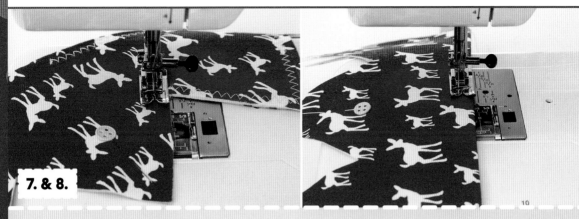

7. & 8.

Now it's time to pin the points of the crown together.

Line up the edges of all the points as best you can. Don't worry if they are a bit messy or have interfacing peeking out. We can trim everything later. Pin the points together.

Once you have pinned all the points together, sew with a fun decorative stitch all the way around the crown. Make sure the ribbon is out of the way and doesn't get caught up in the stitching.

9.

Once you have finished sewing, use a sharp pair of scissors to trim any overhanging interfacing or loose threads. Use the ribbon to tie on your crown.

The great thing about this crown is that not only is it reversible, it is also adjustable to fit all head sizes. Yay!

PAPER OPTION

Want to make this out of paper?

It's easy with just a few simple steps!

What would I need?

* 1 piece of card stock or poster board
* 24″ of fun ribbon, ½″–1″ wide
* Stapler
* Scissors

1 Instead of cutting the crown pieces from fabric, cut 1 piece from card stock. You could pick a fun holiday pattern that would look cute!

2 Cut the ribbon pieces for the ties.

3 Staple the ribbon to the ends of the card stock crown.

Ta-da! How easy is that?

Santa and His Helpers Barrette

what do i need?

* Fat quarter of wool felt
* Large snap barrette
* Heavy spray starch
* Hot glue gun
* Yarn

special skills

* Using a hot glue gun (page 23)
* Making a pom-pom (page 27)

PREPARE the Pieces

* Use the Santa and His Helpers Barrette patterns (page 55) to trace and cut the felt hat cone and base.

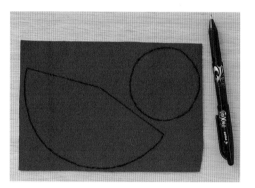

LET'S Make It

1.

Spray both sides of the hat pieces with heavy starch spray until they are quite damp. Then iron them on the wool setting until the starch dries. This should make both pieces pretty stiff—we want our little hat to maintain its shape!

This *super-sweet* hair accessory will have you whistling a holiday tune and channeling your inner Santa (or elf!). The perfect Christmas morning barrette!

2. Gently fold the hat edges in to create a cone shape.

3. Apply a line of hot glue along an edge.

4. Lay the other edge on top, slightly overlapping and covering the glued edge to create a cone shape.

5. Apply a small line of glue along the inside edge of the bottom of the cone.

6. Gently place the cone on top of the felt circle. The circle will be bigger than the base of the hat cone. After the glue has dried, trim off the outside of the circle where it's bigger than the base of the hat cone.

FINISH Up

Let's add a pom-pom! Wondering how to make one? Check out Making a Pom-Pom (page 27).

1. Use a small dot of hot glue to attach the pom-pom to the top of your hat.

2. Once that glue is dry, use hot glue to securely attach the barrette to the hat.

Once it's dry, rock your new holiday hair accessory. Don't stop at Santa; make a batch for all your elf friends.

PAPER OPTION

Want to make this out of paper?

It's easy with just a few simple steps!

What would I need?

* 1 piece of card stock or poster board
* 1 long barrette
* Scissors
* Hot glue gun

Add the barrette and the pom-pom and rock your new holiday look!

1 Instead of cutting the Santa hat pieces from felt, cut them from a piece of card stock.

2 Form a cone with the main hat piece and glue it together with a line of hot glue.

3 Attach the cone to the base with hot glue.

4 Cut away any excess paper from the base.

Santa and His Helpers Barrette
Hat base

Cut 1 from felt.

Santa and His Helpers Barrette
Hat top

Cut 1 from felt.

Neon Tree Forest

what do i need?

* 10 sheets of 8½″ × 11″ colored printer/copier paper

* Parchment paper to make template

* Stapler

* Paper scissors

special skills

* Making a pom-pom (page 27)

PREPARE the Pieces

* Use the Neon Tree Forest pattern (pullout page P1) to trace and cut a parchment-paper tree template.

LET'S Make It

1.

Fold up the corner of a piece of paper to meet the other edge of the paper. The folded area will now be a square. Don't worry about the excess; it won't get in the way!

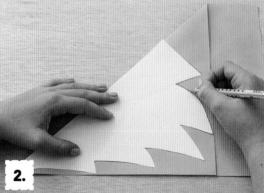

2.

Place the tree template with the straight edge on the fold and trace around it.

Make the perfect centerpiece or holiday bedroom decor with these easy-as-can-be paper neon trees. *Make one or make a whole forest of fun!*

With just a few supplies that you probably already have at home, you can turn a stack of printer paper into a sweet fir forest.

3.

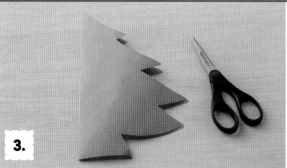

Cut out the tree.

4. & 5.

Follow Steps 1–3 with all the paper pieces until you have 10 paper trees cut out.

Open all the trees and lay them on top of each other. Make sure they are lined up well,

6.

Staple through all the layers at the top and bottom of the tree.

7.

Carefully open all the tree sections so that they are evenly spaced. You may need to fold a few backward. That is okay; you need to do that to fluff out the tree!

8. Make a pom-pom (page 27) for the top of the tree in a fun holiday color.

Make a few trees or make a whole forest! You can even shrink down the pattern piece and make some baby trees too.

Take your time
and ask for
help

Totally Joyful Joy Banner

what do i need?

* ½ yard of felt for banner pieces
* ¼ yard of felt for letters
* 10″ × 14″ of fusible web
* Extra-wide double-fold bias tape
* Yarn
* Basic sewing supplies

special skills

* Using pins (page 22)
* Sewing around a corner (page 22)
* Using an iron (page 23)
* Using fusible web (page 25)
* Making a pom-pom (page 27)

PREPARE
the Pieces

* Using the Totally Joyful Joy Banner pattern (on pattern pullout page P2), trace and cut 4 banner pieces.

* Using the Totally Joyful Joy Banner patterns (pages 64 and 65), trace the letters onto the paper side of the fusible web.

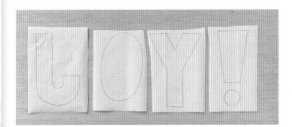

* Iron the fusible web to the felt for the letters.

* Cut out the letters from the felt.

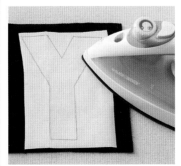

It's hard not to feel the joy when you hang this super-cute Totally Joyful Joy Banner—make it in Christmas colors or any color you choose to bring joy all year-round.

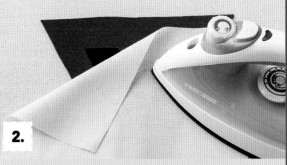

1.

Peel the backing paper from the letters.

2.

Position each letter in the center of a banner triangle. Place a pressing cloth over the top of the letter and iron each letter until it is securely attached to the banner piece.

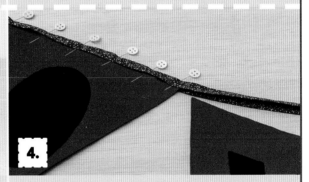

3.

Thread the sewing machine with thread in the same color as the felt letters. Sew around the letters with the presser foot close to the edge.

4.

Lay the double-fold bias tape out on a flat surface, with the opening facing up. Position each banner piece inside the fold of the bias tape.

 note

It's okay if you decide not to stitch the letters, although they may not stay in place over time.

5.

Carefully pin each banner piece in place.

6. & 7.

Thread the sewing machine with thread in the same color as the double-fold bias tape and sew down the open edge, sewing nice and close to the edge. It's important to keep the pieces securely pinned inside the fold.

Make a pom-pom for each of your banner pieces using 40–50 yarn wraps (see Making a Pom-Pom, page 27).

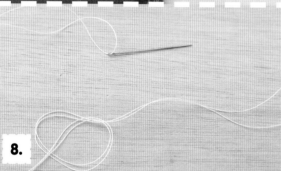

8.

Thread a needle with an arm's length of button thread. Tie a knot a few inches from the end of the thread.

9.

Bring the needle through the felt from behind at the point of a banner piece.

10.

Push the needle through the center of the pom-pom.

11.

Push the needle back through the pom-pom and tie the thread in a double knot with the tail end of the thread. Repeat for each banner piece.

Don't just stop at red and white! Think about some other holiday colors that make you feel joyful. Now find a fun spot to hang your joyful banner and spread the joy!

PAPER OPTION

Want to make this out of paper?

It's easy with just a few simple steps!

What would I need?

* 4 pieces of red card stock for main banner pieces

* 4 pieces of black card stock for letters

* Glue stick

* 1½ yards of ribbon, ¼″ wide

* Hot glue gun or stapler

* Scissors

1 Instead of cutting the banner and letter pieces from felt, cut them from card stock. You could change up the color of the card stock or even use a patterned card stock.

2 Use the glue stick to attach the letters to the banner pieces.

3 Lay the banner pieces out and then place the piece of ribbon across the top. Position the ribbon so that the letters are in the center and the same amount of ribbon comes off each end.

4 Use a hot glue gun or a stapler to attach the ribbon to the banner pieces.

All done! Now go hang it somewhere lovely!

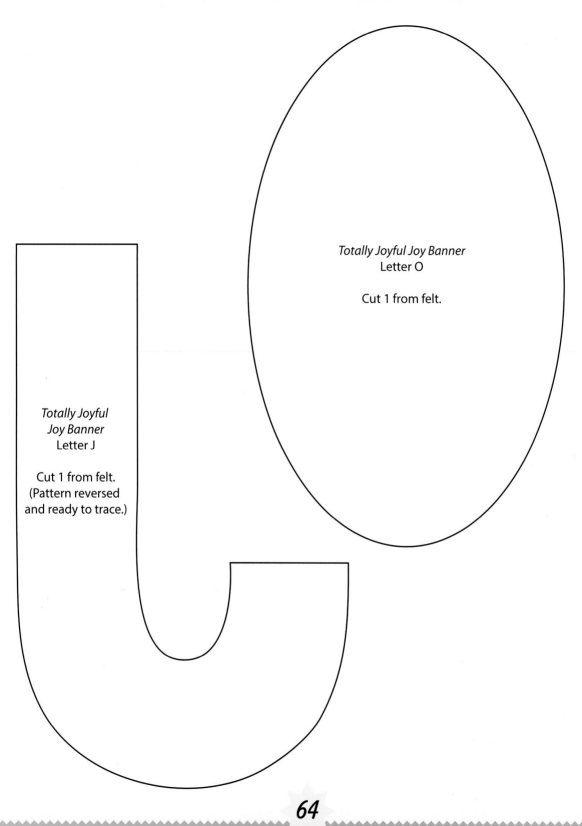

Totally Joyful Joy Banner
Letter O

Cut 1 from felt.

*Totally Joyful
Joy Banner*
Letter J

Cut 1 from felt.
(Pattern reversed
and ready to trace.)

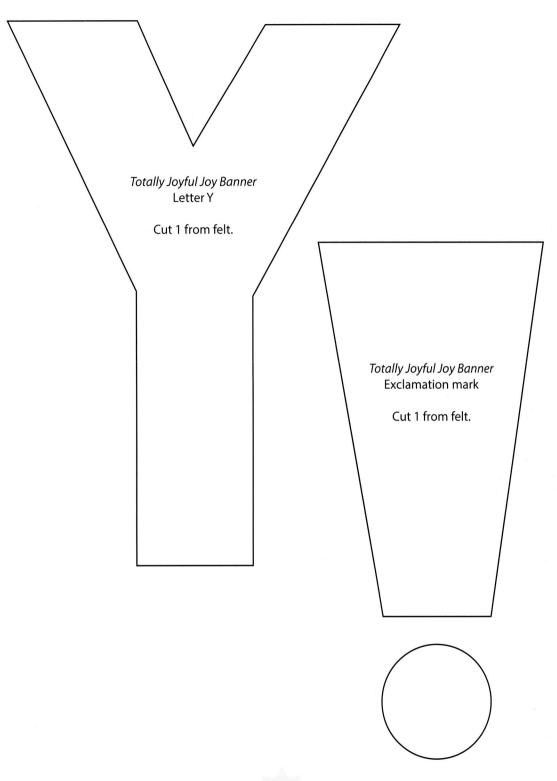

Totally Joyful Joy Banner
Letter Y

Cut 1 from felt.

Totally Joyful Joy Banner
Exclamation mark

Cut 1 from felt.

Stenciled Advent Calendar

what do i need?

* 48 pieces 5˝ × 6˝ each of various holiday prints for bags

* 13½ yards of approximately ¼˝-wide ribbon

* Black fabric paint

* Sponge paintbrush or foam pouncer

* Simple letter stencils

* Cotton twine or clothesline

* Pinking shears (*optional*)

* Basic sewing supplies

special skills

* Using pins (page 22)

* Sewing around a corner (page 22)

* Using an iron (page 23)

LET'S Make It

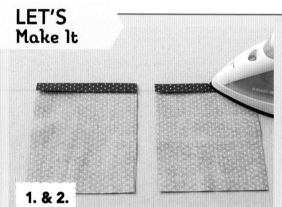

1. & 2.

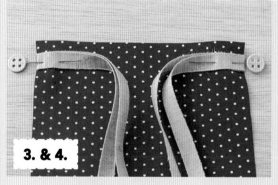

3. & 4.

Divide the bag fabrics into 24 pairs.

Take 1 pair. On 1 of the pieces, fold in the 5˝ edge ½˝ toward the wrong side and press with the iron. Do the same thing with the other piece of bag fabric.

Cut 2 pieces of ribbon 10˝ long and fold them in half so they are 5˝ long.

With the right side facing up, pin ribbon ¼˝ from the folded edge on both sides. Make sure they are pinned so they are facing inward.

tip

It may help to pin the ribbon ends to the center of the fabric piece, so the ends don't get stuck inside the seam allowance.

You will love counting down to Christmas with this easy and original Advent calendar. Each pocket is big enough to store a super-fun and yummy treat.

If you are using a ¼″ presser foot, don't forget to use washi tape as a guide to make the correct seam allowance width for this project (see Seam Note, page 29).

Stenciled Advent Calendar

5.

Place the bag pieces right sides together. Pin down both sides.

6.

Sew with the edge of the presser foot on the edge of the fabric.

7. & 8.

Turn right side out and press well with an iron.

Repeat Steps 2–7 for all the bag pieces to make 24 bags.

LET'S
Stencil It

1. & 2.

Place a piece of scrap paper inside the bag.

Prepare your fabric paint and get your stencil sponge ready.

 tip
Practice stenciling on a piece of scrap fabric until you are happy with the look.

- For bags with just one number (1, 2, 3, 4, 5, and so on), center the stencil on the bag. For bags with two numbers (10, 11, 12, and so on), center both stencils on the bag.

- For bags with two numbers, stencil the first number and let it dry for a little while before you stamp the second number. Maybe stencil all the first numbers first and then go back and stencil all the second numbers!

3. – 5.

Hold the stencil firmly and, with your other hand, use an up-and-down motion to apply the paint to the stencil. You only need a little paint on the brush!

Let the paint dry for a couple of hours; then iron over the numbers to set the paint.

Tie the lovely treat bags to the twine and hang it somewhere in your home!

Woodland Mushroom Wreath

what do i need?

* Foam wreath form

* Hot glue gun

* Stiff double-sided fusible interfacing (such as Phoomph)

* Approximately ⅓ yard of festive colored fabric

* Fabric or felt scraps for mushroom and trees

* Plastic deer or other animals

special skills

* Using a hot glue gun (page 23)

* Using templates (page 24)

PREPARE the Pieces

* Cut long strips from your fabric. I like mine to be about 1″–1½″ wide and as long as the full width of the fabric from selvage to selvage (page 31).

LET'S Make It

Apply a little dab of hot glue to the end of a fabric strip and start wrapping the fabric tightly around the foam wreath. Be sure to overlap each time you wrap.

When you get to the end of the fabric strip, use another dab of hot glue to secure the end of the strip.

1. & 2.

Add another strip of fabric and continue wrapping the wreath until you have completely covered the foam.

3.

69

Nothing says the holidays like a beautiful wreath on your front door. This festive woodland wreath combines two of my favorite things, deer and mushrooms, and it just screams handmade holiday. You may just need to make another one for your bedroom door.

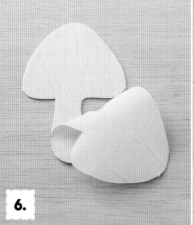

4. & 5.

6.

Using the patterns (page 72), trace the mushroom designs onto a piece of paper.

Cut out the paper shapes and trace around them onto the paper side of the interfacing.

Cut out the interfacing shapes and, once you have chosen the mushroom felt or fabric colors, peel off a side of the interfacing and stick it down on the felt or fabric.

tip Phoomph or stiff interfacing is really useful to make small shapes stiffer. We don't want floppy mushrooms, right?

7.

8.

Cut around the interfaced shape with a sharp pair of scissors.

Now peel the paper off the other side of the shape and stick it to the same color felt on the other side.

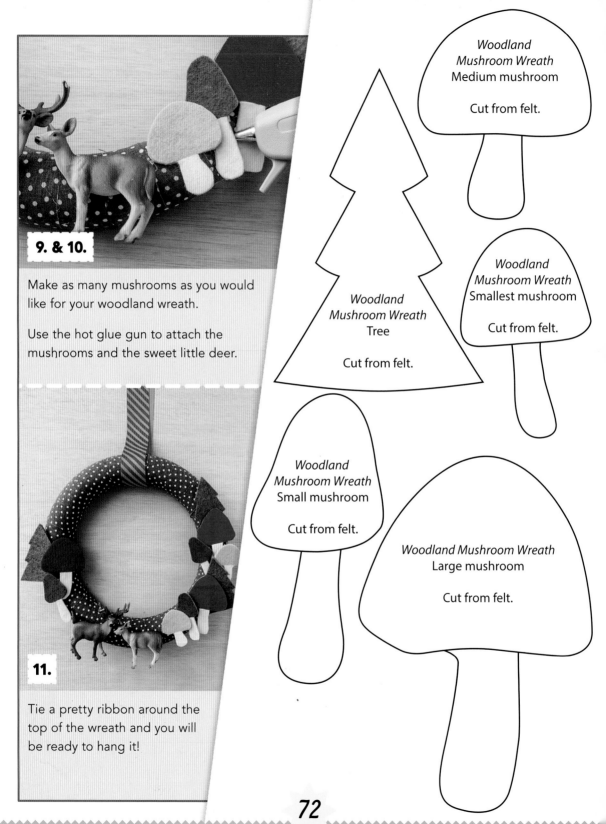

9. & 10.

Make as many mushrooms as you would like for your woodland wreath.

Use the hot glue gun to attach the mushrooms and the sweet little deer.

11.

Tie a pretty ribbon around the top of the wreath and you will be ready to hang it!

Woodland Mushroom Wreath Medium mushroom

Cut from felt.

Woodland Mushroom Wreath Tree

Cut from felt.

Woodland Mushroom Wreath Smallest mushroom

Cut from felt.

Woodland Mushroom Wreath Small mushroom

Cut from felt.

Woodland Mushroom Wreath Large mushroom

Cut from felt.

72

Mistletoe Felt Wreath

what do i need?

* Foam wreath form
* 25″ × 40″ of wool felt
* Approximately ½ yard of fabric to match color of felt leaves
* White yarn
* Hot glue gun
* Heavy spray starch

special skills

* Using a hot glue gun (page 23)
* Using an iron (page 23)
* Using templates (page 24)

PREPARE
the Pieces

* Cut long strips from your fabric. I like mine to be about 2½″ wide and as long as the full width of the fabric from selvage to selvage (page 31).

LET'S
Make It

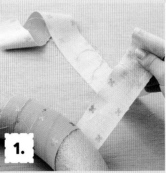

1.

2. & 3.

Apply a dab of hot glue at the end of a strip and start wrapping the fabric around the foam wreath. Make sure it is overlapping and that you are keeping it nice and taut.

When you get to the end of the strip, secure it with a dab of hot glue.

Start with the next strip and continue wrapping the fabric. Continue like this until the entire wreath is covered.

Mistletoe is not only for smooching under! This mistletoe wreath is the perfect winter door decor, and—let's face it—who doesn't love a wreath with pom-poms? Using the same fabric-wrapped wreath technique as for the Woodland Mushroom Wreath, we can create a fun and unique spin on the traditional!

1.

Using the patterns (pages 77 and 78), trace the mistletoe leaves onto tracing paper. Cut out the leaves and trace around them with an erasable pen on the felt. Move them around a little to fit as many as you can on the felt.

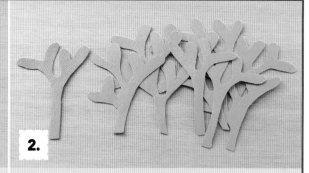

2.

Cut out the mistletoe pieces. Cut 3 leaves from each template for a total of 9 leaves.

3.

Saturate both sides of the felt pieces with heavy spray starch. Set the iron to the wool setting and iron both sides of the felt pieces until they dry and stiffen. If you are using synthetic felt, be sure to set the iron to a synthetic setting and use a pressing cloth.

THE BERRIES

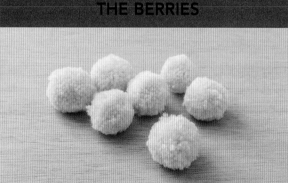

Make about 7 small pom-poms (page 27) for the mistletoe berries. We want them to be small and firm, so keep on trimming until they are nice and berrylike!

 tip The smaller you trim the pom-pom, the thicker it will become.

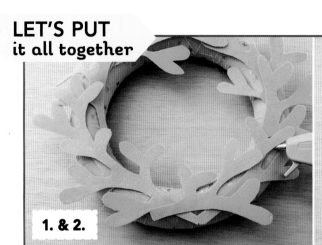

1. & 2.

Apply a line of hot glue to the stem of the mistletoe and attach it to the top of the wrapped wreath.

Apply another mistletoe leaf, overlapping the first leaf.

3.

Continue adding leaves, overlapping each time, until you have totally covered the wreath. You can cut more or fewer leaves depending on how full you want the wreath to look.

4. & 5.

Use the hot glue gun to apply as many pom-pom berries as you think would look best.

Hang the wreath from a pretty ribbon and admire your hard work.

You deserve a little kiss for all that work!

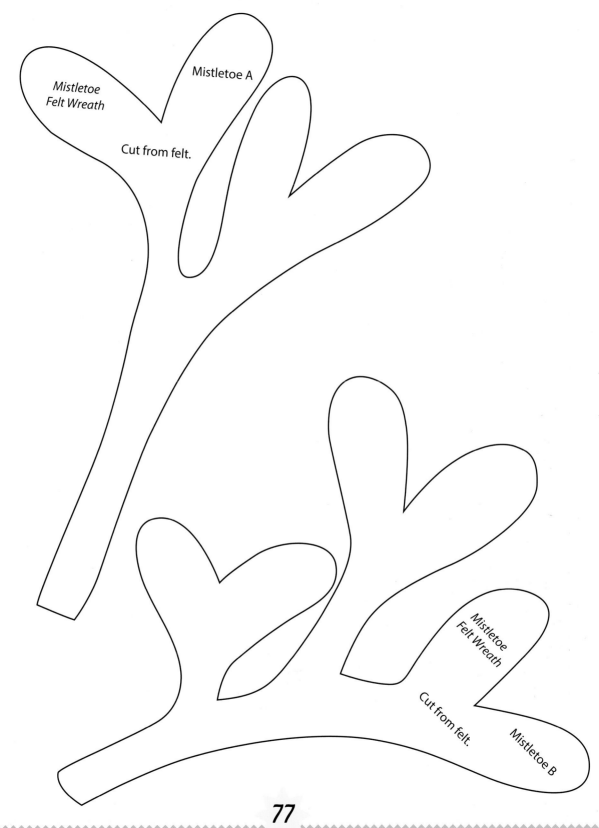

Mistletoe
Felt Wreath

Mistletoe A

Cut from felt.

Mistletoe
Felt Wreath

Cut from felt.

Mistletoe B

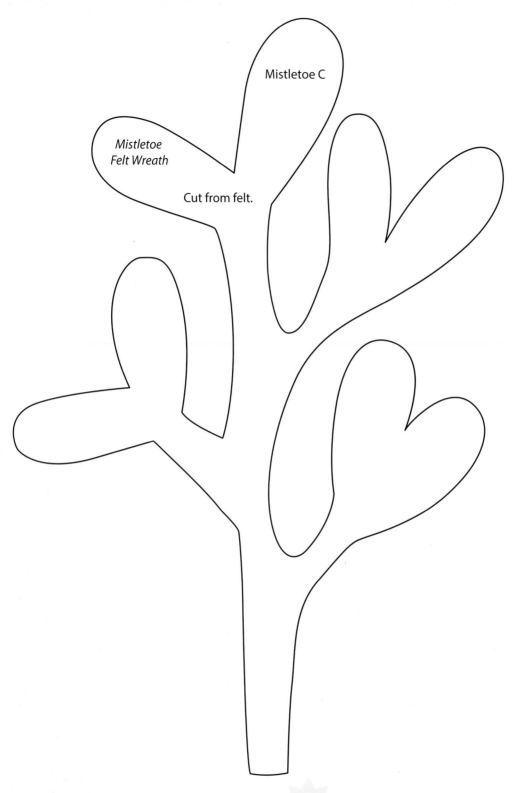

Mistletoe C

Mistletoe Felt Wreath

Cut from felt.

Holiday Dream Catcher

what do i need?

* 9″–12″ embroidery hoop

* Approximately ⅓ yard of festive fabric

* Hot glue gun

* Colored yarn

* Felt scraps

special skills

* Using a hot glue gun (page 23)

* Using templates (page 24)

PREPARE
the Pieces

★ Cut long strips from your fabric. I like mine to be about 1″ wide and as long as the full width of the fabric from selvage to selvage (page 31).

LET'S
Make It

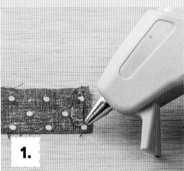

1.

Apply a dab of hot glue to the end of a fabric strip and attach it to the wood embroidery hoop.

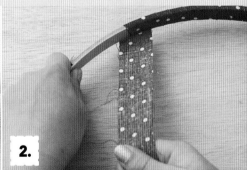

2.

Start wrapping the fabric strip around the embroidery hoop, making sure to overlap with each wrap.

Who needs bad dreams when it's holiday time? *Keep your dreams super sweet* and full of sunshine and rainbows with this fun dream catcher. Make one for each of your pals, so the people you love all have sweet dreams.

3. & 4.

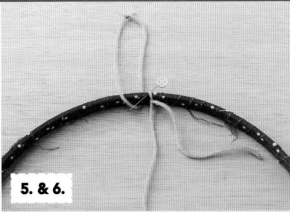

5. & 6.

When you get to the end of the fabric strip, apply some hot glue and attach the next strip. Continue doing this until the entire hoop is covered.

Attach 5 pins to the ring at 5 equally spaced points around the hoop. This is your guide to make the catcher part of your dream catcher.

Cut a 10″ piece of yarn or twine and tie a loop around the top of the hoop. This will be the hanging loop.

Tie the end of a 48″ piece of yarn or twine in a double knot under the hanging loop.

7.

Pull the yarn taut over the first pin and wrap the yarn around the hoop and through the first section.

8.

Now pull the yarn taut to the second pin and wrap the yarn around the hoop and through the next section.

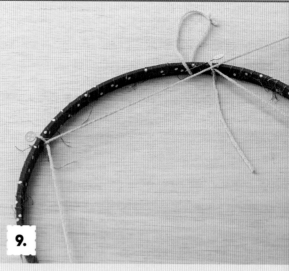

9.

Continue doing this until you have completed the first round in the hoop.

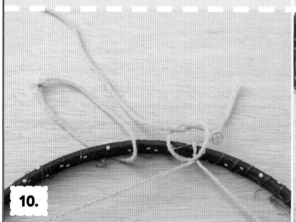

10.

Tie a double knot with the yarn and cut the end.

11. & 12.

Cut another piece of yarn approximately 30˝ long.

Tie a double knot with the new piece of yarn in the center of one of the taut pieces of yarn.

tip Look at the photos if you get a little confused. Sometimes I think it's easier to look than to read with this project.

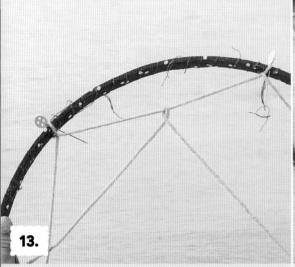

13.

Pull the yarn over to the center of the next piece and wrap it around and through, just like you did before.

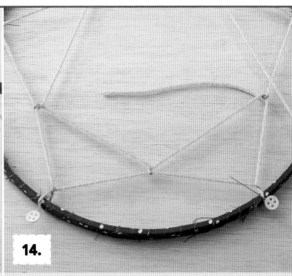

14.

Continue to do this around the entire hoop until you are back to where you started.

15.

End with a double knot.

You can stop here or you can create an inner star in the same way as you did the last star.

Look at the photos to see how.

Always remember to finish this part with double knots.

FINISH
Up

1.

Make a few multicolored pom-poms (page 27) to hang off the bottom.

2.

Use the pattern (page 85) to cut a few feathers from felt. Once you have cut the feather shapes, use a sharp pair of scissors to create the fringy edges of the feathers. I find it helps to draw a line down the center as a guide to making my fringing even.

3. & 4.

Cut a few different lengths of yarn and tie them to the bottom of the dream catcher.

Tie the yarn ends tightly around the pom-poms. Secure them with double knots.

5.

Apply a little dab of hot glue to the yarn ends and attach to the felt feathers.

Great job! Now start dreaming sweetly this holiday season.

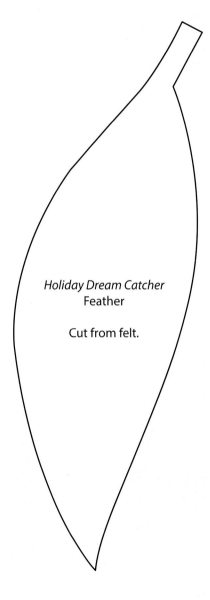

Holiday Dream Catcher
Feather

Cut from felt.

Take your time
and ask for
help

Stitchy Striped Christmas Stocking

what do i need?

* Various sized strips
  of fabric measuring
  anywhere from 1½″ to
  3″ wide and 15″ long

* 10″ of ribbon, ½″–1″ wide

* 15″ × 20″ piece of
  backing fabric

* 15″ × 40″ piece of
  lining fabric

* 15″ × 40″ piece of
  cotton batting

* Basic sewing supplies

special skills

* Using pins (page 22)

* Using an iron (page 23)

* Using templates (page 24)

PREPARE the Pieces

* Use the pattern (on pullout page P1)
  to cut 1 piece of fabric for the backing,
  2 pieces of fabric for the stocking lining,
  2 pieces of batting, and 1 piece of
  parchment paper.

LET'S Make It

THE STOCKING PIECES

If you are using a ¼″
presser foot, don't
forget to use washi
tape as a guide to
make the correct seam
allowance width for
this project (see Seam
Note, page 29).

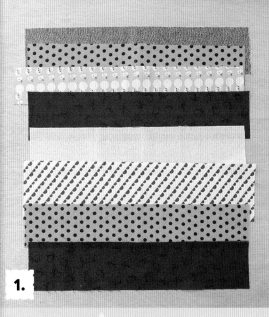

1.

Lay out the strips
of fabric and
arrange them in
whatever layout
you like best.

You will never buy another Christmas stocking from the store once you know how to make your own *fun and stitchy patchwork Christmas stockings.*

Stitchy Striped Christmas Stocking

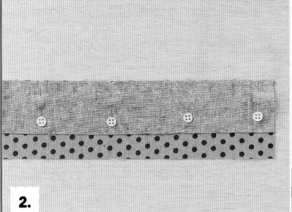

2.

Place the first 2 strips right sides together, making sure that the edges are lined up correctly. Pin along the long edges.

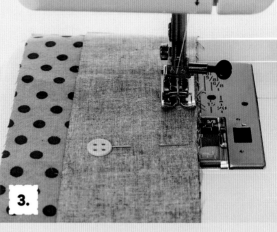

3.

Sew with the edge of the presser foot on the edge of the fabric.

4.

Open out the strip and press really well with the iron.

5.

Attach the next strip in the same way.

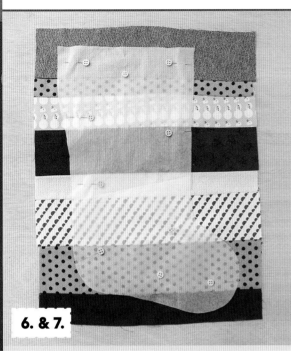

6. & 7.

Continue adding strips until the finished panel measures 19″ long. Give the finished panel a good press with the iron.

Pin the parchment paper template to the strippy panel and cut out the front stocking piece.

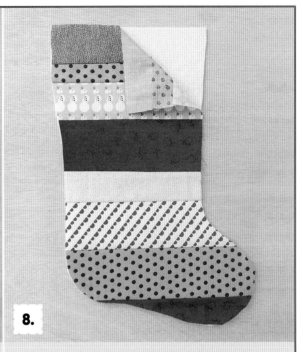

8.

Lay the batting piece on a table and place the strippy stocking front on top it, with the right side facing up.

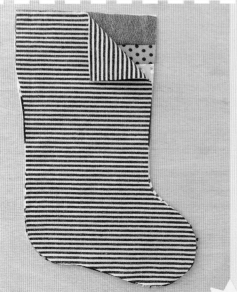

9.

Lay the stocking back piece facedown on top of the stocking front piece.

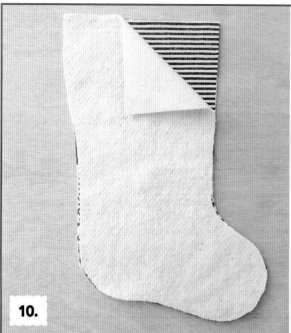

10.

Finish the sandwich by laying the other batting piece on top.

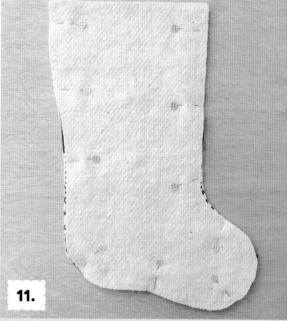

11.

Pin all around the stocking, making sure to leave the top open.

LET'S PUT
it all together

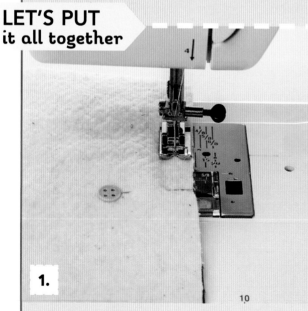

1.

Sew with the edge of the presser foot on the edge of the fabric, making sure to backstitch at the beginning and end.

2.

Clip the curves (page 30) around the heel and the toe of the stocking.

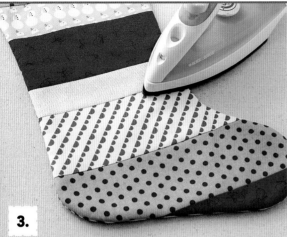

3.

Turn the stocking right side out and press well with the iron.

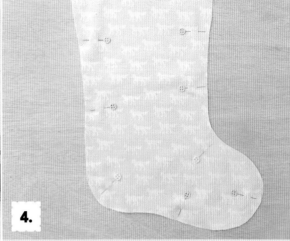

4.

Place the lining pieces right sides together. Pin all the way around, making sure not to pin across the top.

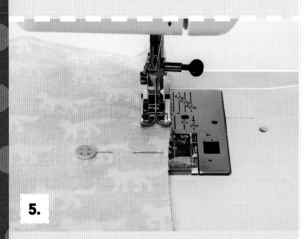

5.

Sew with the edge of the presser foot on the edge of the fabric.

Don't forget, once again, to backstitch at the end.

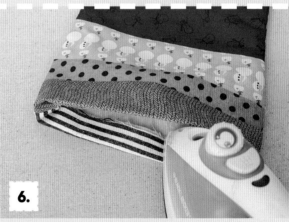

6.

Fold the top of the main stocking inside approximately ½˝ and press well with the iron.

7.

Keeping the lining piece inside out, fold over the top to the outside ½″ and press well with the iron.

8.

Slide the lining stocking inside the main/outer stocking and line up the tops.

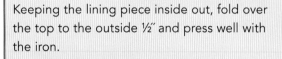

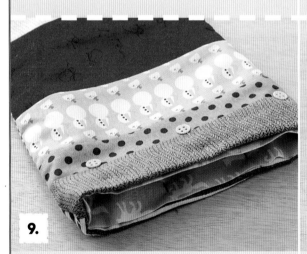

9.

Pin around the top.

10.

Fold the piece of ribbon in half and slide it into the back of the stocking. Slide it down about 1″. Pin in place.

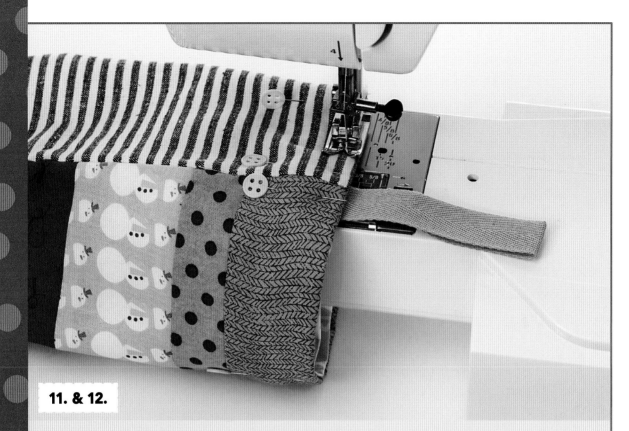

11. & 12.

Carefully pull the extension table from your machine. Does your sewing machine have an extension table attached? On some machines, it's longer like a table, and on others it's a smaller part you may have to take off to get to the bobbin. Check your machine's manual to see what this piece looks like, and how to remove it. You'll need to remove it for the rest of this project to work, because you are sewing something round.

Slide the open Christmas stocking onto the machine and sew all the way around the top edge of the stocking with the edge of your sewing machine's foot on the edge of the fabric. You will know when you are done because you will be back where you started.

Now go hang your stocking on the fireplace and hurry back to bed. You don't want to get caught by Santa!!

Take your time
and ask for
help

Peaceful Dove Pincushion

what do i need?

* 10″ × 10″ piece of white felt

* Small scraps of felt for hat and beak

* Erasable pen (I use FriXion erasable markers because they erase with the heat of an iron.)

* Hot glue gun

* Fiberfill stuffing

* Basic sewing supplies

special skills

* Using pins (page 22)

* Using a hot glue gun (page 23)

* Using templates (page 24)

If you are using a ¼″ presser foot, don't forget to use washi tape as a guide to make the correct seam allowance width for this project (see Seam Note, page 29).

PREPARE the Pieces

* Use the patterns (page 101) to cut all the pieces of your dove.

LET'S Make It

1.

Referring to the pattern, mark an eye on each body section with an erasable pen.

2.

Thread a needle with black embroidery thread and tie a knot around 4″ from the end of the thread. Bring the needle through the eye spot from behind the felt.

My favorite holiday bird may just be the dove. *Doves look so lovely and regal with their all-white coats of feathers.* This project will teach you how to make your own peaceful and regal dove pincushion. It's the perfect home for all your sewing pins and needles. It could also be the cutest ornament in town!

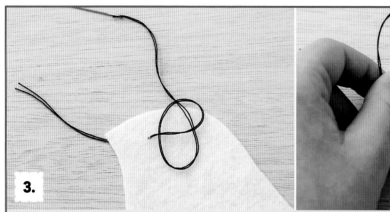

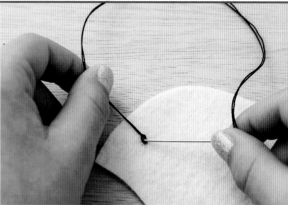

3.

Tie a knot in the thread and, with the point of the needle on the eye spot, ease the knot down the needle so that it is as close to the felt as you can make it.

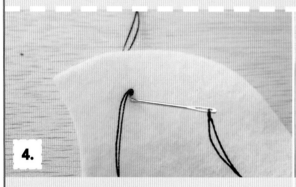

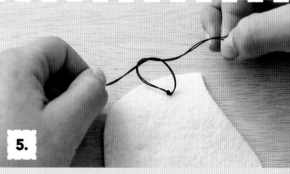

4.

Push the needle down through the felt beside the knot.

5.

Tie a double knot in the thread using the needle thread and the thread tail.

Turn the crown right side out and carefully press all the edges with the iron.

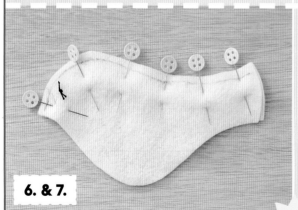

6. & 7.

Repeat Steps 2–5 to make an eye on the other body section.

Place the 2 upper bird body pieces right sides together and pin around the top curve. Use an erasable pen to draw a stitch line ⅛″–¼″ from the edge of the felt. It will really help with this little sewing project.

96

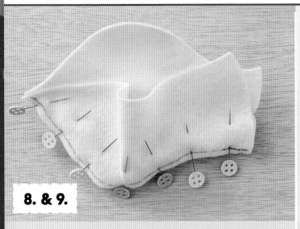

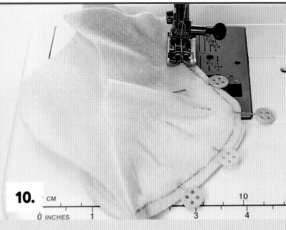

8. & 9.

10.

Sew only the top curve along the drawn line.

Line up a side of the first bird body with the side of the bird belly and pin together. Draw a stitch line again with an erasable pen.

Carefully sew along the line.

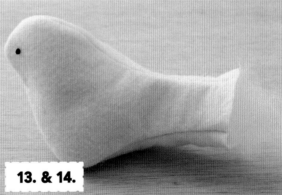

11. & 12.

13. & 14.

Attach the other side of the bird to the other side of the belly in the same way. Be sure to leave the tail open.

Turn the entire bird right side out.

Stuff with small tufts of fiberfill stuffing.

Sew the tail closed with the edge of the presser foot on the edge of the fabric.

 tip I like to use my pinking shears to snip the bird tail to give it a more feathery look.

97

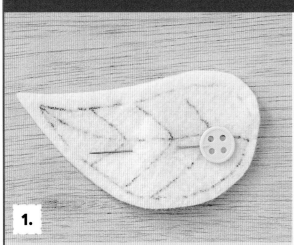

1.

Using the pattern as a guide, draw the detail onto 1 side of each of the wings with an erasable pen. Pin the 2 wing pieces together.

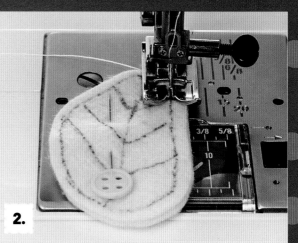

2.

Stitch along the drawn lines in a soft color.

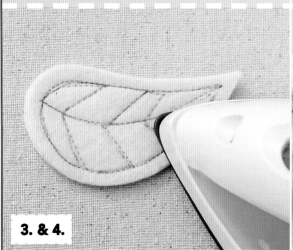

3. & 4.

Do the same thing with the other wing pieces.

Use the iron to remove the pen marks when you are done.

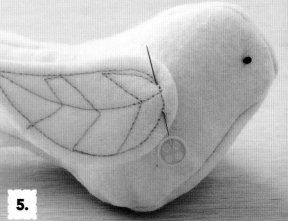

5.

Position the wings on each side of the body and pin in place.

6.

Carefully hand stitch the wings in place around the curve with a simple **whipstitch**, which is a super handy hand stitch used to join 2 pieces of fabric together.

Here's how to whipstitch:

Thread a sewing needle and then tie a knot at the end of the thread.

Bring the needle up from behind the bird wing. Push it down through the main bird body piece fabric that you are attaching. Try to make your stitches nice and small and make sure that each stitch is beside the last stitch.

Bring the needle up and through the edge of the wing again, and then back through the bird body again.

Continue like this until the wing pieces are attached. Sew a couple of stitches in place to secure the stitching. Push the needle through to the back of the wing and tie a knot close to the fabric.

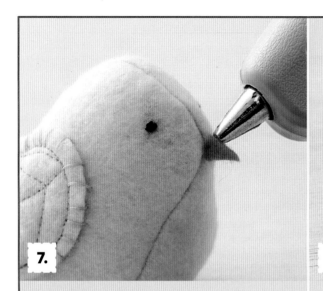

7.

Cut the felt beak and attach it to the bird with a drop of hot glue.

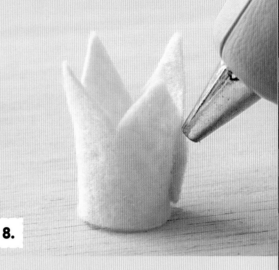

8.

Use a dab of hot glue to secure the crown in a round shape.

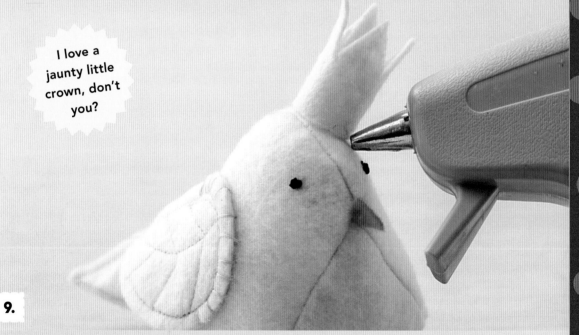

I love a jaunty little crown, don't you?

9.

Use another dab of hot glue to attach the crown to the bird.

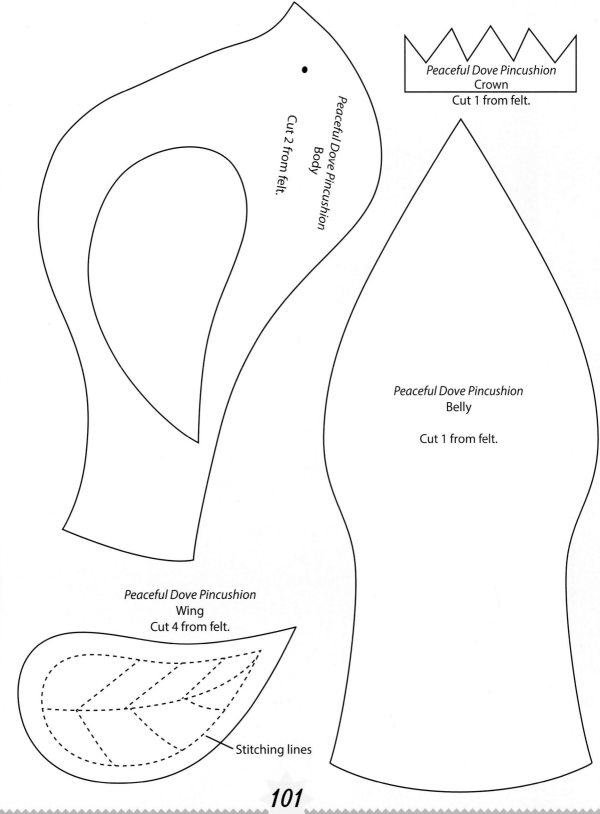

Peaceful Dove Pincushion
Crown
Cut 1 from felt.

Peaceful Dove Pincushion
Body

Cut 2 from felt.

Peaceful Dove Pincushion
Belly

Cut 1 from felt.

Peaceful Dove Pincushion
Wing
Cut 4 from felt.

Stitching lines

101
Peaceful Dove Pincushion

Pom-Pom Poinsettia Magnet

what do i need?

* 2 pieces of bright and festive card stock (The larger piece should be at least 7½″ × 7½″.)

* 1 pom-pom (page 27)

* Ruler

* Stapler

* Magnet

* Erasable pen or pencil (I use FriXion erasable markers because they erase with the heat of an iron.)

* Hot glue gun

special skills

* Using a hot glue gun (page 23)

* Making a pom-pom (page 27)

PREPARE
the Pieces

* Use the pattern pieces (pages 106 and 107) to cut 1 large circle from card stock and 1 smaller circle from card stock. Also cut the two smallest (center guide) circles. We will be using them as guides for cutting.

LET'S
Make It

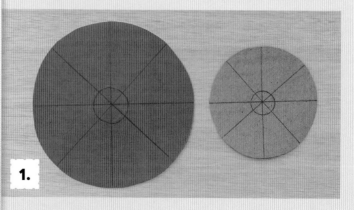

1.

Use an erasable marker and a ruler to divide the circles into 8 even segments. Use the smaller circles to draw a circle in the center of the card stock circle. This will be the guide to show you where to stop cutting.

102

Turn the idea of a classic holiday poinsettia into a fabulous paper poinsettia magnet. A little bit of folding and you can have your own *colorful folded poinsettia garden!*

Pom-Pom Poinsettia Magnet

2.

Snip each segment with a sharp pair of scissors, making sure to stop at the marked center circle. Do this with both circles.

3.

Carefully fold the corners of each segment toward each other and secure with a staple or hot glue.

4.

It's going to look like you are creating a little cone on the end of each segment.

Don't be tempted to crease the paper; you want to form a rounded cone.

Do this with each of the segments, on both circles.

5.

Use hot glue to attach the smaller flower on top of the larger flower. You only need to glue at the center.

6.

Add a fun pom-pom with hot glue.

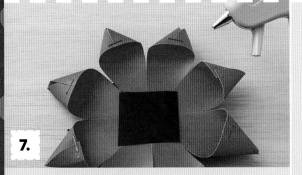

7.

Attach a magnet to the back with hot glue.

Make a few and adorn any magnetic surface with a holiday bloom fest!

Pom-Pom Poinsettia Magnet
Large flower

Cut 1 from cardstock.

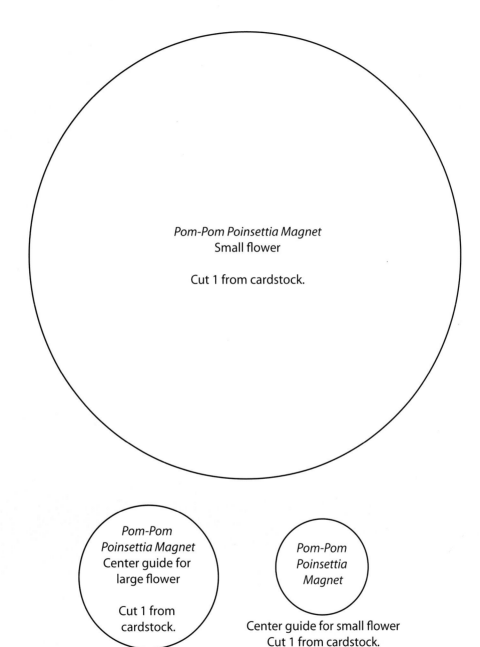

Pom-Pom Poinsettia Magnet
Small flower

Cut 1 from cardstock.

*Pom-Pom
Poinsettia Magnet*
Center guide for
large flower

Cut 1 from
cardstock.

*Pom-Pom
Poinsettia
Magnet*

Center guide for small flower
Cut 1 from cardstock.

A teeny bit more challenging

Sweet Felt Cutout Ornament

what do i need?

* 8″ × 12″ piece of white felt for background

* 8″ × 12″ piece of colored felt for design

* Fusible web

* Fun-colored thread

* Ribbon, ¼″–½″ wide

* Basic sewing supplies

special skills

* Using pins (page 22)

* Using an iron (page 23)

* Using fusible web (page 25)

PREPARE
the Pieces

* Using the pattern (page 112), cut 2 circles from white felt.

* Using the pattern (page 113), trace 2 ornament design pieces onto the paper side of a piece of fusible web. (You trace 2 ornament designs because the ornament has 2 sides.)

Channel your inner Scandinavian with this Nordic-inspired neon felt ornament. Super simple and easy to make, this ornament will certainly brighten up your tree!

1.

Iron the fusible web design to the piece of felt.

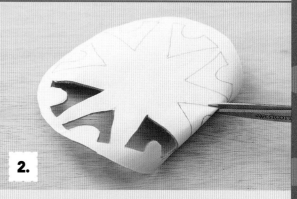

2.

Use small, sharp scissors to cut out the design.

3.

Peel off the backing paper from the design piece of felt and position it centered on the white circle.

4.

Iron the design piece to the felt circle.

> ⭐ **tip** If you are using synthetic felt, be sure to use a pressing cloth. You do not want the iron to melt your beautiful design.

5. & 6.

Using a fun-colored thread, sew close to the edge of the entire design. You can use an erasable pen to mark a stitch line, if you like.

Repeat Steps 1–5 for the second circle.

7.

Fold a piece of ribbon in half and position it on the wrong side of 1 of the circles, about 1″ down from the circle edge.

8.

Lay the circles wrong sides together and pin together.

9.

Sew all the way around the circles with white thread. It's a good idea to sew nice and close to the outside edge.

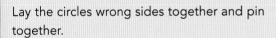

Make these to top a gift or to decorate your tree.
You can even enlarge or reduce the size of the design
using a photocopy machine or computer scanner.

PAPER OPTION

Want to make this out of paper?

It's easy with just a few simple steps!

✂

What would I need?

* 1 sheet of white card stock

* 1 sheet of fun colored card stock

* Glue stick or hot glue gun

* Scissors

1 Instead of cutting the felt ornament pieces from felt, cut them from card stock. You could change up the color of the card stock or even use a patterned card stock.

2 Use a glue stick or hot glue gun to attach the cutout piece to the plain circle.

3 Do the same with the other side.

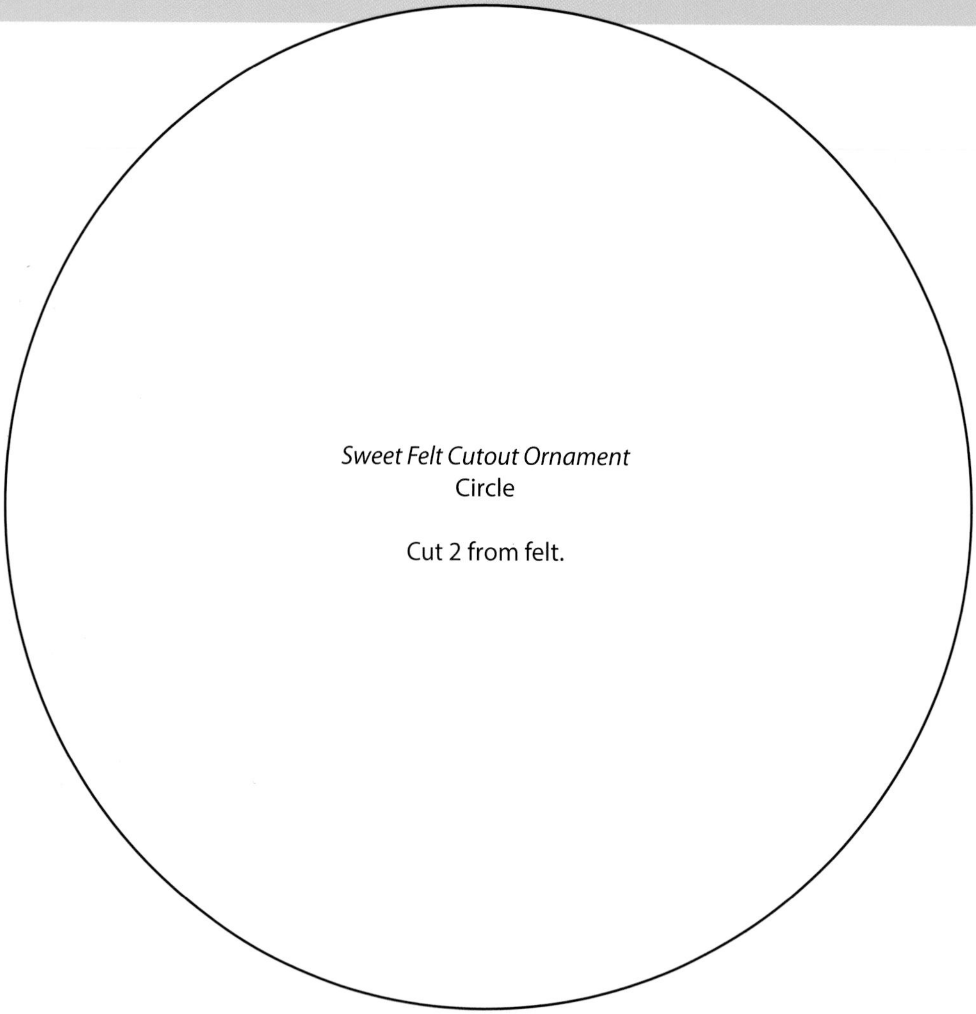

Sweet Felt Cutout Ornament
Circle

Cut 2 from felt.

4 Hot glue the ribbon to the wrong side of 1 of the circles.

5 Hot glue both of the circles together.

How easy was that? Now make a whole ton of these and decorate your tree!

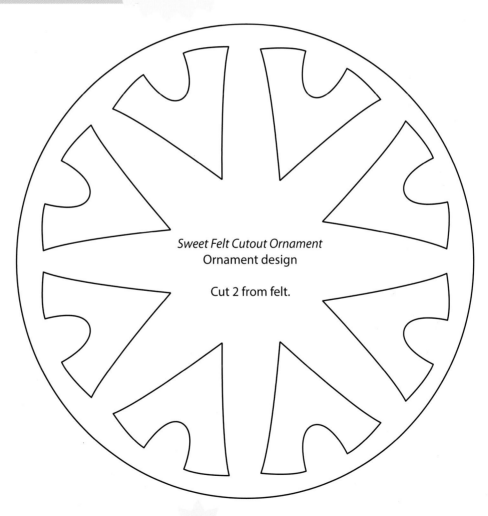

Sweet Felt Cutout Ornament
Ornament design

Cut 2 from felt.

Easy peasy

Wordy Art Noel

what do i need?

* Cardboard letters from craft store

* Festive fabric

* Felt

* Ruler

* Fabric or tacky glue

* Cotton batting

* Erasable pen (I use FriXion erasable markers because they erase with the heat of an iron.)

* Basic sewing supplies (*optional*)

special skills

* Clipping the curves (page 30)

LET'S Make It

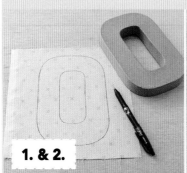

1. & 2.

Lay the first letter face-down on the wrong side of your choice of festive fabric. Trace around the outside of the letter with an erasable pen.

Do the same with the other side of the letter.

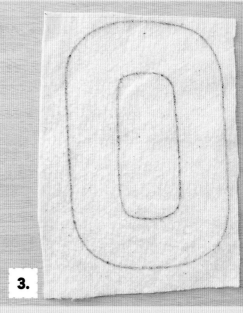

3.

Do the same with the cotton batting.

Did you know that the word *Noel* is another word for Christmas? Make your own gorgeous Noel letters using easy-to-find supplies and set them up on the mantelpiece this holiday season. *You will have so much fun making them* that I just know there will be many more words you will want to make all year-round!

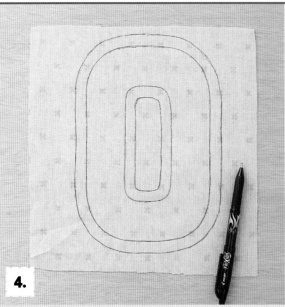

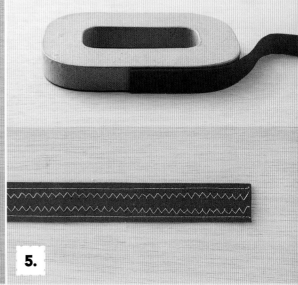

4.

Before cutting out the letter from the fabric, draw another line around the letter that is about ½″ outside the line you have just traced. The letter will be much neater if the fabric can fold over the edges a bit.

5.

Measure the width of the edges of the letter and cut strips of coordinating felt this width.

Option: Thread the sewing machine with a fun-colored thread and do some crazy stitching on the felt side strips.

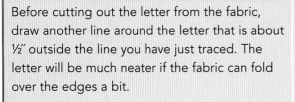

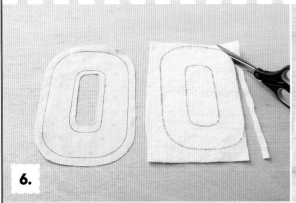

6.

Cut around the outer line on the festive fabric and the drawn line on the batting.

7.

Use a sharp pair of scissors to clip the curves only up to the traced line of the letter on the festive fabric.

116

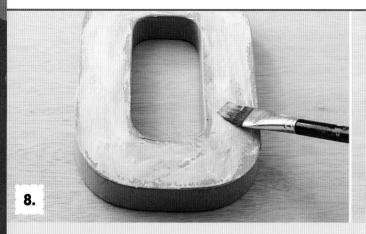

8.

Apply some tacky glue to the letter and attach the batting on the front and back.

Apply some glue around the edge of the letter.

9.

10.

Lay the fabric on top and wrap the fabric edges around the letter edges.

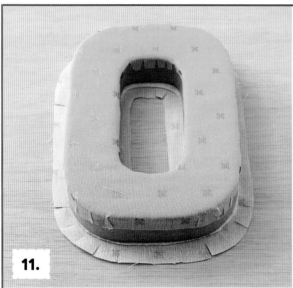

11.

Do the same thing with the other side of the letter.

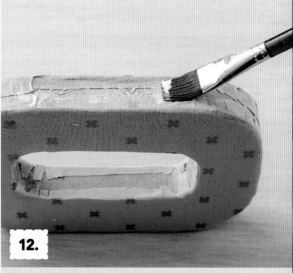

12.

Apply some glue around the edges of the letter.

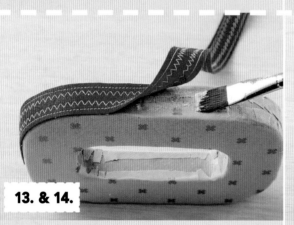

13. & 14.

Carefully glue down the felt edging.

Repeat Steps 1–13 for the rest of the letters.

Imagine how fun these will be in all different fabrics! Make a whole shelf of holiday words for yourself and those you love!

PAPER OPTION

Want to make this out of paper?

It's easy with just a few simple steps!

What would I need?

* Cardboard letters
* Pieces of patterned paper
* Tacky glue
* Scissors

1 Instead of tracing the letters onto fabric, you can trace them onto the wrong side of the patterned paper. Follow the fabric pattern for cutting directions. (We are not using batting for this, so you will only need to trace onto the paper.)

2 Attach the letters to the paper with tacky glue. Don't forget to attach the paper to both sides of the letter!

3 Instead of the felt strip around the outside, you can again use patterned (or plain) paper. Simply cut a strip from paper and glue it on with tacky glue.

Holiday Menagerie Animal Ornaments

what do i need?

* Hot glue gun

* Scraps of felt

* Erasable pen (I use FriXion erasable markers because they erase with the heat of an iron.)

* Fun-colored embroidery thread

* Tiny bells

* Plastic toy animals

* Basic sewing supplies

special skills

* Using a hot glue gun (page 23)

* Using templates (page 24)

PREPARE the Pieces

* Use the patterns (page 125) to cut all the pieces for the animal costumes.

* Measure your animal's belly. Cut a piece of felt ½˝ wide by the length of the belly measurement for the main waistband.

* Cut the same for the inner waistband. Use a different color felt for this, and keep in mind that we will be cutting the edges down with pinking shears.

tip All the animals will have different-sized bellies! Be sure to measure each one before you cut the felt!

LET'S Make It

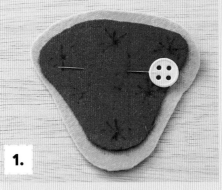

1.

Use an erasable pen to draw some stars around the inner saddle felt piece. Lay the inner saddle piece on top of the outer saddle piece and pin in place.

When you think of holiday ornaments, I bet you never think about a holiday safari! Think outside the box with these cheerful traveling festive animals. Don't just limit yourself to a giraffe; *why not throw a horse or even a kitty into the mix?*

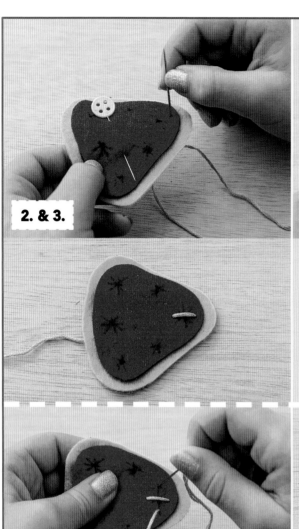

2. & 3.

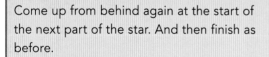

Thread a needle with a fun and festive colored embroidery thread. Tie a knot at the end.

Bring the needle up from behind the felt at an end of the star. Push the needle down through the felt at the other end of the line of the star.

4.

Come up from behind again at the start of the next part of the star. And then finish as before.

Keep doing this until you have finished all the stars.

5.

Use pinking shears to cut a decorative edge along the inner waistband piece.

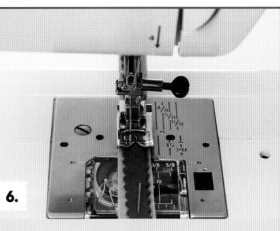

6.

Attach to the wider waistband using the sewing machine and a fun colorful zigzag stitch.

7.

Use a needle and embroidery thread to attach a mini bell to each side of the saddle. Simply bring the needle up from behind the edge of the saddle.

8.

Push the needle through the little hole on the bell.

9.

Tie a double knot with the thread tail and the thread in your needle.

10.

Attach the other bell in the same way.

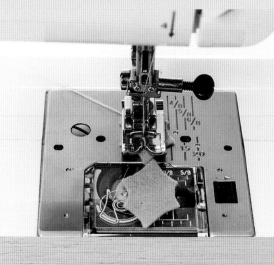

11.

Attach the saddle and waistband to the animal with some hot glue.

FINISH Up

Cut the holly pieces from green felt and sew them together in a line with the sewing machine, using a straight stitch. Start sewing down the center of the first holly piece. Before the needle can sew off the end of the piece, add another piece. Keep attaching them like this until you have a long string of holly.

Wrap the holly garland around the neck of your animal and then start on another … I love the idea of a whole herd of holiday friends!

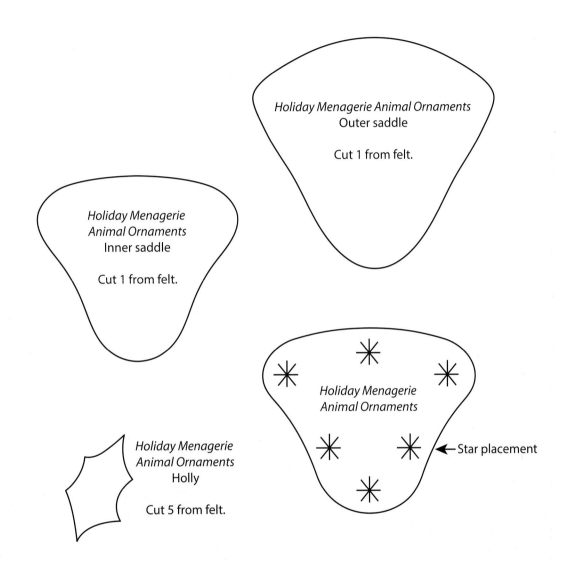

Holiday Menagerie Animal Ornaments
Outer saddle

Cut 1 from felt.

*Holiday Menagerie
Animal Ornaments*
Inner saddle

Cut 1 from felt.

*Holiday Menagerie
Animal Ornaments*

← Star placement

*Holiday Menagerie
Animal Ornaments*
Holly

Cut 5 from felt.

ABOUT THE AUTHOR

Annabel Wrigley is an Aussie mom, author, designer, and owner of Little Pincushion Studio in Warrenton, Virginia. Her studio is a gathering place for crafty little pixies who want to learn everything they need to know about sewing and crafting. Her books *We Love to Sew*, *We Love to Sew—Bedrooms*, and *We Love to Sew—Gifts* are helping children all over the world to channel their inner craftiness and embrace the wonderful world of sewing. Visit her website at littlepincushionstudio.com.

Also by Annabel Wrigley

About the Author

FunStitch
✕ ✕ ✕ ✕ ✕ ✕ ✕ ✕ ✕ ✕
STUDIO

FunStitch Studio books are written and designed specifically with kids, tweens, and teens in mind!

"Every time I finish a project, **I get so excited**, because I feel like I can do **anything!**"
—Annalise, age 12

The text and projects are age appropriate and *nurture the love of handmade* in budding sewists, quilters, embroiderers, and fashion designers.

by Rachel Low

by Brenna Maloney

by Maryellen Kim

See the complete list of FunStitch Studio titles at ctpub.com/funstitch-studio

an imprint of C&T Publishing

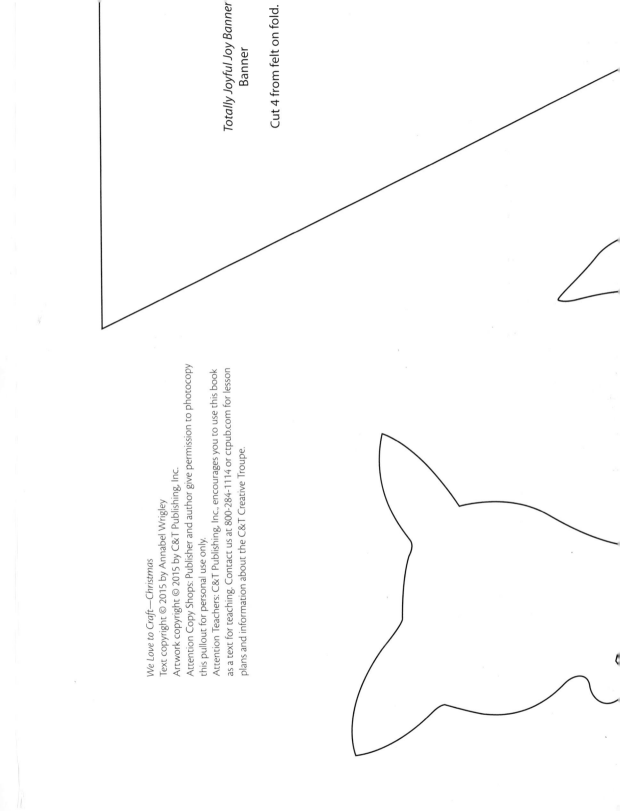

Totally Joyful Joy Banner
Banner

Cut 4 from felt on fold.

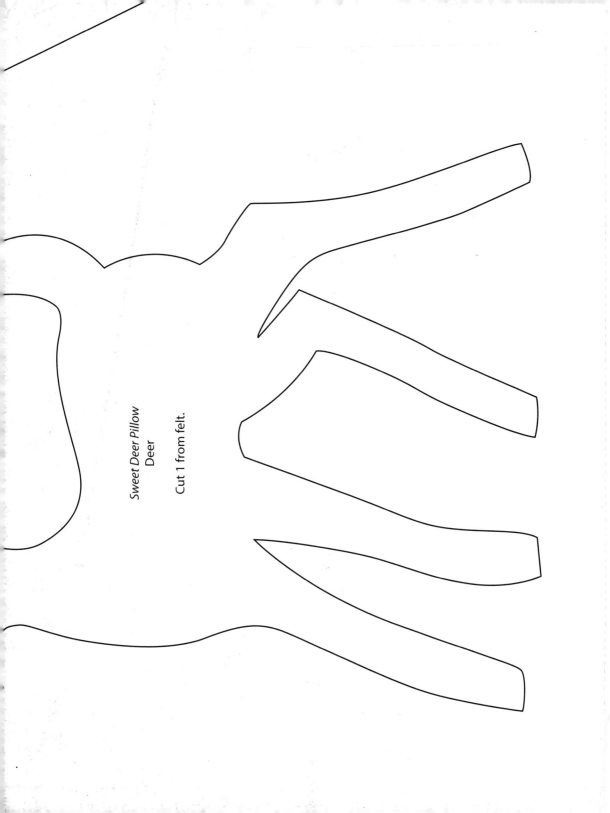

Sweet Deer Pillow
Deer

Cut 1 from felt.